Work Life Bal
Prot

By,
Bhatia,Yoge
eta

ACKNOWLEDGEMENT

The brief acknowledgements mentioned here are not enough to thank all those who contributed importantly in this research work. My trust in God is a constant driving force in my life and has a great deal to do with the completion of this doctoral work and writing this thesis.

First and foremost I take this opportunity to thank my guide Prof. Srilatha, who has been an exceptional supervisor. She has been instrumental in developing my self-confidence to conduct this research. Her powerful in-depth knowledge of the subject area has shown me the light ahead during the course of this work. As for me, I am totally indebted to her and will remain so for the rest of my life.

My guide is also the Director of SOMS, and inspite of her very busy schedule and work pressure as the Director of the school, she has always given me her precious time to see the progress of my work at each step. I am excited at the prospect of submitting my thesis at a time when my guide, Prof. Srilatha is the Director of SOMS.

Each faculty of SOMS, IGNOU has helped me a lot during this research. I would like to especially thank Dr. Gopal for being very supportive throughout my period as a researcher in IGNOU, and guiding me with the nuances of the system. Also I would like to extend my thanks to Mr.Shwet who helped me when I was drowned in numbers.

I would like to express my deepest gratitude towards Prof. Gopa Bhardwaj and feel extremely honoured to have presented my synopsis, seminars, and pre-submission before her as the subject expert. Her perfection and scholarliness in the subject area has helped my research see the light of the day.

I express my thanks to Indira Gandhi National Open University (IGNOU) for absorbing me as a research scholar. I would like to extend my special thanks to the non-academic staff members at SOMS, Ms. Mukta, Mr. Anand and Ms. Vandana, who facilitated the co-ordination for me. I would like to convey my very special thanks to the Librarian, Mr. Imam for helping me with accessing the relevant journals, publications, and going about the search for existing studies.

Data collection was one of the most crucial tasks in this study. This research work owes its unconditional support to all the respondents for sparing their precious time.

Last but not the least, I would like to express my deepest gratitude to my family: my husband Dr. Nishant, whose continuous support made this research work possible. He motivated me throughout this research work and extended his support physically, emotionally, and intellectually. A very special thank you to my child, Shiven, who is the purpose of my life, and because of him I took on this endeavour and completed it successfully. Finally I would like to thank my (late) father, grandmother, and grandfather Shri Siri Ram Jolly who all made me capable of reaching here.

CONTENTS

LIST OF TABLES

ignou   Work –Life Balance among Women Professionals

LIST OF FIGURES

CHAPTER- 1
INTRODUCTION

INTRODUCTION

Over past few years, the topic of Work life balance (WLB) has gained increasing importance, as excessive demands of work have been perceived to represent an important issue. The main influences that the topic of WLB has mostly dealt with are- work domain and its influence, personal domain or life outside work, and factors affecting both-whether individual factors or organizational factors. Due to changing work requirements over the years, these influences have changed and pressures related with work have increased due to various factors like more information that needs to be handled, requirement for quick response, prompt customer support requiring rapid adjustments. (Guest, 2002)

The term 'work-life balance' broadly includes the interplay between different variables that denote the day-to-day management of paid work and other non-work activities. WLB is thus often used as an overarching and all inclusive term, and is the subject of recent international research work, policy determinant, focus of multidisciplinary conferences and commonly appearing theme in the titles of books and journal articles (Crooker, Smith and Tabak 2002; Glubczynski, Kossek and Lambert 2003).

Researchers in a variety of fields such as medicine, management, academia, HR or corporate have tried to assess and analyse employee work-life balance.(Wilk, 2013) Since there is high degree of subjectivity as WLB is individual experience related concept, its precise definition has varied and remained abstract. (Ironson, 1992). However, despite the inherent subjectivity and individual experience based variations, WLB merits a thorough investigation, along its different dimensions as the outcome and sequelae of low balance or 'imbalance' or less than satisfactory work life balance, can be intense and may include job burnout and stress which

ignou   Work –Life Balance among Women Professionals

negatively impacts individuals personal and professional lives, and their job and life satisfaction (Beauregard & Henry, 2009).

Defining and Conceptualizing the Work-Life Relationship

Academic literature, especially recent research, gives significant attention to the concepts 'Work-life balance' and 'Work-life conflict' (Hayman, 2005; Pocock, 2005). The two terms 'work-life balance' and 'work-family balance' are generally believed to denote the same concept, although these two terms are used interchangeably (Bell, 2012). 'Work-life balance' has been used in this research work, since the term 'life' is more inclusive than 'family' as it incorporates work, personal and family responsibilities (Bell, 2012, Sarkar, 2011).

Researchers have defined Work-Life Balance (WLB) as 'satisfaction and good functioning at work and at home with a minimum of role conflict' (Clark, 2000). According to Greenblatt, it may be sometimes characterised by 'the absence of unacceptable levels of conflict between work and non-work demands' (Greenblatt, 2002). Conversely, if there is an incompatibility between the two domains, that is, work and non-work, due to their respective demands, conflict may occur. Hence work-family conflict or work-non work conflict imply incompatibility between two domains or lack of balance. (Frone et al, 1997; Parasuraman et al, 1996). Such conflict can occur both when work roles interfere with non-work roles and vice versa.

Researchers have described five main models to explain the relationship between work and life outside work. (Zedeck and Mosier, 1990). According to the segmentation model, work and non-work are two distinct domains of life. These two are lived separately and do not affect or influence each other. However, this model appears to bed mainly theoretical as empirical evidence supporting it is rather limited. (Guest,2002). On the other hand, according to the spillover model, the two domains influence each other either positively or negatively. Although there is evidence supporting spillover, the model itself is a generalized perspective of the influence of two domains on each other, and adds limited value (Guest,2002). The third model or compensation model suggests complementary nature of the two domains. It hypothesizes that demands or satisfactions lacking in one domain can be made up in the other, such as an un-demanding work causing unsatisfaction, which is compensated for more challenging activities such as major role in community services outside work.

Fourth model or instrumental model, focuses more specifically in terms of one domain facilitating success in other. An example of this model is the instrumental worker, who would work long hours to increase earnings to facilitate more success in non work domain like purchase of a car or home. The fifth model is a conflict model, which proposes that since both domains require time, the demands from both domains may have competing effect rather than complementary effect, resulting in conflicts and increased overload on an individual (Guest, 2002). **Current research work also uses conflict perspective based definition and model to evaluate WLB.**

In the recent years, there has been an interest and focus, mostly on the conflict model. Although spillover and compensation models are also topics of academic enquiry, research on conflict model is reported especially in families where couple is working (Guest, 2002).

Work and personal life have continued to be looked at differently in the literature. However, 'conflict' has been part of the focus, both in past and more so, currently. (Pickering,

2006; Lewis, 2002). Research suggests, both work place and family have their respective demands, which are often exclusive and require time. This requirement of 'own' time by both institutions, leads to incompatibility and conflict. (Pickering, 2006)

There are three components of 'conflict'- time related conflicts, or conflict due to competing time requirements, conflicts associated with strain produced due to competing demands, and behavioral incompatibility related conflict. (Greenhaus & Beutell, 1985). According to Carlson et al., 2000, the concept of work-family conflict includes three-dimensions, that is, time, strain and behavior, and two directions, that is, work-family, family-work.

Work-family conflict occurs when the time, which is a limited resource, can fulfill the requirements of one of the two domains, or when strain arising from involvement in or fulfillment of one role makes it difficult to meet the requirements of another role, or when behavioral incompatibility required in one role make it difficult to meet the requirements of another role (Greenhaus & Beutell, 1985). Thus, work-to-family conflict (WFC) or family to work conflict (FWC), may occur due to involvement in one domain, affecting other domain as a result of time demand, induced strain, or behavioral incompatibility. Based on this view of 'conflict' and perception of low conflict as balance, the terms WLB and WFC are used interchangeably. (Lewis, 2002). Additionally, some researchers prefer use of term "life" to "family" since former also includes experiences of non married or single individuals. (Burke, 2004). Hence the term work life balance or WLB has gained prominence.

The concept of WLB, although discussed in literature, was assumed till recently to be a gender linked concept, leading to more of comparative studies between genders than within each

ignou   Work –Life Balance among Women Professionals

gender (English, 2003; Stephens, 1994). However, several researchers have reported the applicability and importance of concept to both genders and across various levels of professional hierarchy. (Blair-Loy, 2003).

Studies focusing on work and related conditions report increasing levels of stress in professional lives. (Judge & Colquitt, 2004). Thus persistent stress may lower productivity and satisfaction, levels and increase employee turnover. (Porter & Alman, 2010).

Similarly, researchers report trend towards increased amount of time spent on jobs, with some reporting employees working an extra month per year currently, compared to few years earlier. (White, 2003). Overworking can impact WLB, as paucity of time may create inter role conflict. (Bacharach, Bamberger & Conley, 1991; Innstrand, Langballe & Falkum, 2010). In fact, this has led the employees to seek optimal work conditions, and place premium on time availability for non work domain, in process viewing WLB as a success parameter. (Maxwell & McDougall, 2004, Jennings & McDougald). Some variables that may affect WLB are working conditions, financial resources, leisure, family, social participation and health (Warren, 2004). Employees have reported increased levels of burnout and negatively affected well being, in the absence of WLB (Cinamon & Rich, 2010).

At organizational level, recognition of importance of WLB has led to policies such as flextime, facilities for childcare, and other measures that attempt to limit family's interference with work (Rothbard, 2001). Some of the organizational policies and programs may help in alleviating difficulties in work domain, and avoiding burnout and attrition. (Haar & Roche, 2010). The efficacy of such policies may be dependent of supervisor support and understanding (Cinamon & Rich, 2010). Researchers have reported that supervisor's support and leadership skills significantly impacted satisfaction at job, attrition, performance and overall sense of well being. (Purcell and Hutchinson,2007).

People develop different ways to have cope up with both the domains. According to Reynolds, there is a gender difference in how people try to manage two domains. While women try to titrate their working hours and professional lives to manage family lives irrespective of whether work interferes with family or family interferes with work, men titrate their working hours only when work interferes with family. Thus women may end up accommodating on professional front more than men. (Reynolds, 2005)

The Indian Context

Professional participation of educated women in different sectors like technical, managerial etc, has been increasing in India. This increase has been associated with a rise in dual career families. (Komarraju,1997). Indian studies report that due to family responsibilities, Indian women face different challenges from their western counterparts, especially in the morning when going for work, and on returning from work. Family pressure during those times, make boundary management challenging. (Rout, Lewis and Kagan,1999).

Additional challenges faced by women in India, come from relative lack of infrastructure like electricity, water or modern kitchen appliances, which make household chores especially challenging, and 'balance' difficult to attain. (Komarraju, 1997) Often organizations don't have flexible hour options or childcare facilities, which act as additional constraints (Bharat, 2001).

ignou   Work –Life Balance among Women Professionals

In a relatively low gender equality society like India, social and spousal support gain greater importance, as far as WLB is concerned. (Rosenbaum and Cohen, 1999). However, although spousal support is adequate as far as participation in job is concerned, spousal support in domestic responsibilities is rather limited, for Indian women. (Ramu, 1989).

A common mode of instrumental support in India are the hired domestic helps. Despite the fact that these helps are often expensive, they still are a common and useful support for nuclear families. (Sekaran, 1992). Despite social, legal and economic reforms, unequal distribution of domestic responsibilities, and unaltered perceptions of society leads to greater conflict in women managers as compared to their male counterparts. (Bharat, 2003). Thus due to cultural, social, and economic factors, genders perceive and respond to WLB differently in India, compared to their western counterparts.

Personal Factors affecting WLB

Interconnectivity between work and family domains, and meeting the obligations of both domains can impact WLB. (Edwards & Rothbard, 2000; Md-Sidin, et al., 2008). Although stress has been studied at length, the definition of stress has varied widely. Conflict acts as a stressor, similar to other stressors like role ambiguity, and lack of perceived control, and can lead to negative outcomes like dissatisfaction, anxiety, psychosomatic symptoms and absenteeism. (Jex & Gudanowski,1992). Several personal factors like gender, marital status, parental status, family responsibility, age, personality differences and education level can lead to or aggravate the imbalance.

Gender

WLB and its association with gender has been extensively studied. Women may take part time jobs to maintain their professional skills, get additional source of income and maintain social life outside house. (Warren, 2004) However, this may also result in impaired WLB (Drew, 2005; Innstrantd, Langballe, Falkum, 2010). Additionally, shouldering of most of the child upbringing responsibilities, may lead to conflict and in turn to burnout and dissatisfaction at job. (Porter & Ayman, 2010).

Prioritization also differs in genders, men sacrificing mostly along family domain if required, and women mostly sacrificing along work domain if required. (Haworth & Lewis, 2005; Jennings & McDougald, 2007). Thus although women may maintain their job involvement, career progression and satisfaction may get negatively impacted. (Hall & Richter, 1988, Martins, Eddleston and Veiga 2002)

Marital status

Married individuals give time or priority to their family life (Martins, Eddleston & Veiga, 2002). Marital life may make it different to separate the boundaries between work and family life resulting in spillover resulting in negative impact on both domains (Hall & Richter, 1988). Thus married individuals may experience more negative impact on WLB than unmarried ones. (Md-Sidin, 2008).

Parenthood

ignou   Work –Life Balance among Women Professionals

The presence or absence of children in the family may negatively impact WLB in individual's life. (Tausig & Fenwick, 2001). Parental status may be correlated to parents giving more importance on the family role (Blau, et al., 1998). This is further reinforced by the finding that dual career couples with no children have better WLB or lesser conflict as compared to both couples with children. (Tausig & Fenwick).

Age and Lifecycle

Age and lifecycle are also important variables, with several researchers reporting significant impact of these on WLB. (Wang, Lawler & Shi, 2010). Lifestyle and lifecycle differences are often correlated, since lifestyle preferences differ across generations. Tausig and Fenwick (2001) reported that advanced age or lifecycle were associated with better WLB, and overall life satisfaction. This may be due to better financial situation, coping , autonomy, or limiting the effort in maintaining 'balance' by individuals later in their lives, since they may be better placed, and reticent in putting extra effort. (Bardwick, 1986).

Personality

According to Jennings and McDougald (2007), personality traits and types may influence perception of WLB. The ability to emotionally attach or detach, feel guilty or ignore, sensitivity or lack of it, may make it either easier or difficult to manage boundaries, and balance domains. (Bekker, et al., 2010).

Internal or intrinsic focus may help individuals concentrate on evolving themselves and realizing their own potential. They seek and may be able to satisfy their requirement for autonomy, and competence, which may in turn help in attaining balance. (Van den Broeck,

ignou   Work –Life Balance among Women Professionals

Vansteenkiste & Has De Witte, 2010). Such individuals may be open to change, growth and realizing their own creative potential (Ros, Schwartz & Surkiss, 1999, Van den Broeck, Vansteenkiste & Has De Witte). On the other hand, external or extrinsic focused individuals may try to create external impression, and may seek job and financial security to do so, rather than develop themselves. This may negatively impact WLB and be associated with lower job satisfaction. (Van den Broeck, Vansteenkiste & Has De Witte).

Education Level

According to some researchers, higher level of education and greater experience may lead to a sense of self sufficiency and self confidence, resulting in better balance and lesser conflict. (Chong & Ma, 2010). However, contradictory findings have been reported by others, with some studies suggesting greater WLB among those with a high school degree or less, or lesser WLB among those with an undergraduate degree or advanced university degree (Tausig & Fenwick, 2001). Possibly, effect of education is moderated to an extent by individual's personal characteristics, and outlook.

Life Demands

Long work hours and nature of work, may make individuals feel isolated from family and leisure activities and instill a perception of not meeting life's demands on personal or non work domain. (Haworth & Lewis, 2005). Thus life demands like leisure, socializing, time for health, etc, if not met may lead to emotional draining, feeling of being overwhelmed, and lower threshold for development of state of conflict. (Warren, 2004, Boles, Johnston & Hair, 1997).

ignou   Work –Life Balance among Women Professionals

Attempt to moderate one's response to conflict and stress may further create negative emotions and augment stress. (Rothbard, 2001). Thus life demands if not met, may sap energy and create negative affect, lowering balance between the domains. A person experiencing stress may show social withdrawal, and lowered willingness to interact with others. (Adams, King & King, 1996).

Work Related Factors affecting WLB

Employees experience prolonged work-hours, intense work conditions, and dynamic and ever changing environment with less time for settlement.(Haworth & Lewis, 2005). Such demanding work conditions, have been associated with anxiety and reduced of job satisfaction (Jex & Gudanowski, 1992). Thus both physical work environment, and psychological work-environment, impact WLB perception. (Gilbreath, 2004).

Job-stress, directly and negatively impacts job satisfaction (Bacharach, Bamberger & Conley, 1991). Job satisfaction is conceived as the degree to which alignment of expectations with reality perception related to job, is achieved. (Bacharach, Bamberger & Conley). Some researchers report that workers displaying high levels of job stress chronically, may be at an increased risk of chronic health problems. (Kang, et al., 2010).

Work Characteristics

The organizational environment comprises of worker interaction, engagement, overall atmosphere and worker orientation with respect to atmosphere and to each other. (Chong & Ma, 2010). Organizational structure comprises of hierarchal make up, division of responsibilities, and autonomy in conjunction with reporting structure. (Chong & Ma). Work related variables in

ignou   Work –Life Balance among Women Professionals

association with organizational structure and environment, can affect WLB. These variables include task related autonomy, working hours, degree of flexibility, supervisor instrumental support, access to and availing of WLB-policies. (Jennings & McDougald, 2007).

Innstrantd, Langballe and Falkum (2010) report that individuals working in jobs or professions that require either regular interaction with others or multiple roles or taking responsibilities for others, may experience impaired WLB. Similarly, at managerial and above levels, task ownership for others as well, may make achieving balance difficult. (Innstrantd, Langballe, Falkum). Sense of injustice or discrimination, may make achieving WLB difficult. (Judge & Colquitt, 2004).

Autonomy

Perceived autonomy with one's role may influence perception of WLB as well. Individuals with perception of lower levels of autonomy over their jobs, are more likely to report conflict and imbalance between work and family roles (Baral & Bhargava, 2010). Less perception of autonomy may also lead to somatic manifestations in the form of chronic illnesses, or impaired mental health. (Bond & Bunce, 2001). Conversely, workers with greater perception of control, report less stress, mental complaints or somatic issues or burnout and attrition. (Bond & Bunce). Perception of greater control also social interactions with coworkers, encourages out of role participation in organizational initiatives, and enhances productive behavior. (Baral & Bhargava).

Technology

ignou   Work –Life Balance among Women Professionals

Studies report both types of influences technology can have on WLB. Technology can both positively and negatively impact WLB. Advancements in technology has helped employers improve efficiency and make themselves more accessible for the client. However, technology has also made employees more accessible even at home so that 'personal' time has decreased, making round the clock working possible. (Maxwell & McDougall, 2004). This change has led to employees working additional hours more frequently. Working more outside of regular office hours has lead to work interfering with family life. Individuals are expected to be always on the job and always accessible (Seron & Ferris, 1995).

Motivation

According to Meyer et al, work motivation is a "set of energetic forces that originates both within as well as beyond an individual's being, to initiate work-related behaviour, and to determine its form, direction, intensity and duration" (Meyer, 2004). Motivation can be driven due to internal factors or intrinsically as well as due to external factors or extrinsically (Meyer, 2004). Intrinsic motivation is driven by individual's own sense of gratification and fulfillments and pursuits to achieve these. New challenges and activities are sought to further one' learning and growth. Extrinsic motivation refers to "the performance of an activity in order to attain some separable outcome" (Meyer, Becker & Vandenberghe). Motivation can influence participation in a domain, and the extent to which an individual may be willing to negotiate boundaries and cope. Thus, it may indirectly influence perception of WLB. (Alexandris, Tsorbatzoudis & Grouios, 2002).

Performance Expectations

ignou   Work –Life Balance among Women Professionals

Performance expectations may influence conflict, more so because of the process followed than end point themselves. Organizations developing targets in keeping with employees progression and future growth potential, may employees in attaining sense of self efficacy. (Chong & Ma, 2010). Additionally, supervisor support received in meeting performance expectations may enhance the individual's sense of purpose and sufficiency. (Gist & Mitchell, 1992). Researchers have established a connection between supervisor's support, feedback, understanding and employee's performance (Chong & Ma). Performance can be improved by the positive and constructive feedback from supervisor at various milestones of meeting performance standards. (Mumford et al., 2002). This may lead to employees valuing their work, an environment of trust, and ease in managing boundaries, and coping. (Chong & Ma)

Organizational Culture

Organizational culture can stimulate employees for meeting higher performance standards. Organizational culture relates to "the assumptions, values, attitudes, and beliefs that are shared among significant groups within an organization" (van Beek & Gerritsen, 2010). Employees derive their identity and direction from organizational culture gives employees identification and direction (Martel, 2002). It is imperative for an organization to be supportive of an employees use of WLB programs, as only then can these programs be successful. Successful implementation can not only improve WLB but also output. (Porter & Ayman, 2010). Thus only a supportive culture can avoid increasing employee discomfort while utilizing the WLB programs (Maxwell, 2005).

Commitment to worthwhile objectives evokes moral motives that can foster satisfaction even in the absence of economic or relational benefits (Meyer & Parfyonova, 2010). Employees

ignou   Work –Life Balance among Women Professionals

may find working in an organization with a strong ideology (one consistent with their own) very rewarding even if other aspects of their daily experiences are not. In other words, they may be willing to make some sacrifices (e.g. turning down more interesting or higher paying jobs elsewhere) and continue to cooperate with the organization because it is the "right" thing to do for the cause (Meyer & Parfyonova).

Constraints

Three types of constraints may affect WLB- structural, intrapersonal and interpersonal. (Godbey, Crawford and Shen, 2010). Structural constraints are external constraints that arise due to lack of availability of resources that are required for participation in a domain and its related activities. (Alexandris, Tsorbatzoudis & Grouios, 2002). Intrapersonal constraints are individual specific and based on one's own evaluation of requirement of participation in a domain,and to what degree. (Godbey, Crawford & Shen). Interpersonal constraints are based on local environment, culture and social norms, and can influence domain participation. (Godbey, Crawford & Shen).

Management of constraints, and gradually overcoming them, can improve perception of WLB. Initial step in managing constraints is the realisation of type of constraint one is facing, and its form such as infrastructure, facilities, lack of social network, and cultural environment. Constraints may influence motivation and participation, if they persist. Hence step wise mitigation, may reduce domain spillover or conflict (Alexandris, Tsorbatzoudis & Grouios, 2002).

Competition

Competition may have both positive and negative impact on WLB perception. On the positive side, it encourages innovation and performance while discouraging complacency. However, it can also have negative effect and along with lack of supervisor support, can create stressful environment, and spillover. Additionally, due to high attrition, burden may be unequally distributed on remaining employees, leading to conflict. (Bloom & Reenen, 2006, White, et al., 2003, Porter & Alman, 2010).

Role Conflict

Role conflict occurs when pressure from two or more domains coincide such that it makes boundary management difficult, and affects role involvement. (Bacharach, Bamberger & Conley, 1991). According to researchers, there are three major forms of conflicts-time based, strain based and behavior based conflict (Greenhaus & Beutell, 1985). Time-based conflict arises when both domains or roles have extensive time demands, resulting in competition over time spent, creating time pressure that leads to incompatibility between the domains, and eventually leads to conflict. Strain and behavioral conflict occur due to stress from simultaneous pressure from both domains, and incompatible behavioral requirements from both domains respectively. (Gilbreath, 2004). Role overload may be the starting point of role conflict eventually leading to WLB along any or all dimensions. (Higgins, Duxbury & Lyons, 2010; Bacharach, Bamberger & Conley, 1991).

According to some researchers WLB can be understood as an interplay and outcome of role overload, role overlap and role incompatibility leading to stress and conflict. (Watkins,

ignou   Work –Life Balance among Women Professionals

1995). An example of role overload and overlap is employees taking work home with them, thus blurring the boundaries between two domains. (Baral & Bhargava, 2010).

Job involvement

Job involvement has been described as "psychological identification with a job" (Kanungo, 1982). Some researchers like Reitz and Jewell (1979) have defined job involvement as the "importance of work in an individual's daily life." Job involvement by itself is a rigorously investigated variable just like work life balance. This is because organizational effectiveness and productivity can be affected by Job involvement, making it an important attitudinal variable that impacts work (Seo,2013). Organizations may be significantly benefited by employees showing high levels of job involvement (Diefendorff, 2002). Thus, Job involvement may be linked with or affect work performance, efficiency and behavior (Yang, 2006)

Social Support

Social support is a consequence of informal social setup that provides offers individuals with instrumental or emotional assistance. (Md-Sidin, et al., 2008). Increased work or non work social support has positive effect on an individual's general health (Adams, King & King, 1996; Md-Sidin, et al., 2008).

Individuals with multiple sources of support manage to alleviate the negative effects of conflict to some extent, and reduce overall work-family conflict (Martins, Eddleston & Veiga, 2002; Cinamon & Rich, 2010). Thus social support augments one's coping mechanism leading to reduction in negative effects of stressors and work-family conflict (Md-Sidin, et al.) Similarly,

ignou   Work –Life Balance among Women Professionals

employers can provide a supportive work environment which may help in stress reduction and improve WLB of their employees. Organizations can be more receptive to employee's family related problems and play a supporting role. (Boles, Johnston & Hair, 1997).

Martins, Eddleston and Veiga (2002) found that to keep employees motivated, and involved, it is important to acknowledge their family domain's existence and the problems it brings along. This can also influence an employee's satisfaction in their career. Researchers suggest that flexible work schedules can make working conditions more supportive. (Boden, 1999). In providing work-life balance programs there is the potential to better support employees (Milliken, Martins & Morgan, 1998). Research has demonstrated that supportive work environment and WLB policies have a positive effect on work-family (Major & Lauzun, 2010).

The supervisor can titrate the demands of the job to make it optimally satisfying. (Gilbreath, 2004). The supervisor can also enable the degree of autonomy an employee gets, so as to maximize employee's sense of accomplishment and achievement. (Purcell & Hutchinson, 2007). Additionally, accommodating stance from supervisor when an employee faces WLB issues, can significantly improve the employee's job satisfaction and positively impact his or her output or productivity. (Gilbreath; Watkins, 1995). Supervisors who are themselves part of a dual career association or marriage, are more receptive and accommodating of employees inter domain conflict. (Watkins).

Thus perception of supervisors as supportive by the employees, improves employees' overall commitment to the organization (Thornhill & Saunders, 1998) and reduces reported levels of stress and work-family conflict (Cinamon & Rich, 2010; Judge & Colquitt, 2004). Working mothers with supportive bosses have reported reduced stress, exhaustion, and tension,

ignou   Work –Life Balance among Women Professionals

apart from spillover (Watkins, 1995). Research suggests supervisor's supportiveness may augment an employees' confidence level, leading to enhanced performance. (Baral & Bhargava, 2010). Harris (2001) reported that a supportive manager shared information and work plans timely, not keeping it for last minute, and also discussed about likely decisions and issues an employee may be facing.

Social support especially non work related support, like the one from family members is however, relatively unexplored variable in terms of its significance with respect to work life balance. Family members are a major source of social support and research suggests positive correlation between social support and individual's health and well being. (Goh, 2015) Additionally while daily work load can positively affect work-family conflict, the effect of work load may be alleviated to some extent by supervisor work-family specific support. (Goh, 2015).

Outcomes

A person's well-being is often assessed within the domains of physical well being, emotional well being, and social well being (McDowell). A person usually spends more time in non work domain as compared to work domain. (Haworth & Lewis, 2005). Thus, the importance of leisure in people's lives should not be underestimated (Haworth & Lewis, 2005). Hall & Richter (1988) argue that the employee needs to have boundary separation and minimal overlap between the two domains else he or she may face burnout and dissatisfaction. There have been many benefits, both at the individual and organizational level, found to be associated with attaining work-life balance.

Professional Outcomes

ignou   Work –Life Balance among Women Professionals

Professional outcomes can both be personal in nature or from the organizational level. Employees experience many positive outcomes due to positive WLB. Employers also are motivated to implement family-friendly policies, as the increase in productivity and lower burnout and attrition, will lead to individual and organizational growth as a result of such policies (Allen, 2001).

WLB programs can create a culture of honesty and trust where staff can admit to home problems and get support (Maxwell & McDougall, 2004). Some benefits with WLB programs and their implementation, at the organizational level are lower burnout, higher productivity (Ulshafer, Potgeisser & Lima, 2005), enhanced quality, employee progression, and lesser absence (Haar & Roche, 2010), increased organizational commitment, increased levels of organizational citizenship behaviors (Baral & Bhargava) and sense of ownership within the organization (Haar & Roche). It has been found that WLB programs allowed supervisors the option to help staff and made the management role less difficult (Maxwell & McDougall).

When an individual leads a balanced life, they are likely to have high energy levels as a component of work engagement (Cinamon & Rich, 2010). Vigor comprises of high levels of pro-activity, ability to persist, and high level of energy. (Cinamon & Rich). Pro-activity on behalf of the employee, can result in benefits both to the individual and the organization (Ruderman, Ohlott, Panzer & King, 2002), thus, employers need to be flexible and supportive to the employees.

There are many consequences associated with lack of WLB. Issues with WLB may lead to stress, burnout, lower organizational commitment, lower job satisfaction, and lower life satisfaction. (Major & Lauzun, 2010). Researchers report that blunting of boundaries, between

ignou   Work –Life Balance among Women Professionals

work and personal life, not encouraging off-time, and by bringing day care, or other family facilities on work place, instead of leaving it in personal domain, may make it more difficult for employees to maintain boundary differentiation and management. (Hall & Richter, 1988). Thus, solution may become problem itself, if not well conceived, or not taking employee preferences into consideration. Since research shows, work interfering with family (WIF) is more common than family interfering with work (FIW), workplace factors and supportive supervisor behaviours play an extremely critical role. (Major & Lauzun).

Personal Outcomes

At the individual level, some benefits that balanced work and life may confer on employees may includes lower conflict, more 'family time' or 'off-time' (Maxwell & McDougall, 2004) and physical and mental well-being (Cinamon & Rich, 2010). Positive or enhanced WLB also enhances the psychological well being of the employees by increasing a sense of self sufficiency and self growth which can lead to positivity towards work (Baral & Bhargava).

Work-family enrichment is the degree to which involvement and gains from one role improve the experiences or enhances the gains in the other role (Baral & Bhargava, 2010). Enrichment is also a consequence of lower spillover of demands to another domain (Porter & Alman, 2010). This may suggest that when people are happier with their work role and family life, they will be more helpful and enjoyable to work with. (DeLong, 1992).

ignou   Work –Life Balance among Women Professionals

Both as dependent and independent variables, job involvement and WLB have been studied. However, there are few studies focusing on the relationship between WLB, job involvement and family support, together. Additionally there are negligible studies in India studying the impact of family support and job involvement on WLB in women professionals, and evaluating the relationship with respect to different sectors, and evaluating the relationships of job involvement and family support with all three dimensions of WLB (time, strain and behavior), and all two direction (work-family, and family -work).

CHAPTER -2
REVIEW OF LITERATURE

REVIEW OF LITERATURE

The concept of work life balance (WLB) finds a wide area of application- in the area of business, and for -profit organizations (Blair-Loy, 2003; English, 2003). According to Hill et al., (2001), work life balance is the degree to which an individual is able to simultaneously balance the temporal, emotional, and behavioural demands of both paid work and family responsibilities.

Definitions

Researchers like Clark et al, 2000, describe WLB as the process of striking an ideal balance between the professional life of an individual and their personal life with all of their respective associations. According to Veenhoven, 1991, an adequate WLB makes a person happier and more content (Veenhoven, 1991). Being content, people maintain the level of hard work they put in their respective careers and might remain satisfied. However, this balance may get affected if, to maximize their achievements, people continue putting in more efforts, thus increasing their working time and losing WLB. Thus, it is widely accepted that continuously maintaining WLB is the current need of the hour.

According to Kalliath & Brough, 2008, "Work-life balance is the individual perception that work and non- work activities are compatible and promote growth in accordance with an individual's current life priorities." Researchers have conceived WLB differently, such as equity across multiple roles (Greenhaus, Collins, & Shaw, 2003), or satisfaction between multiple roles (Clark, 2000; Kirshmeyer, 2000). Thus, an individual's freedom to decide where and how to work and the importance of following own priorities in doing so are emphasized.

ignou   Work –Life Balance among Women Professionals

Researchers have defined and interpreted the concept of WLB differently. Kofodimos et al, 1995, have defined work-life balance as "a satisfying, healthy, and productive life that includes work, play, and love" while Marks & MacDermid, 1996, define role balance as "the tendency to become fully engaged in the performance of every role in one's total role system, to approach every typical role and role partner with an attitude of attentiveness and care. Put differently, it is the practice of that even handed alertness known sometimes as mindfulness" Kirschmeyer, 2000, defined a balanced life as "achieving satisfying experiences in all life domains, and to do so requires personal resources such as energy, time, and commitment to be well distributed across domains", while Clark et al, 2000, define WLB as "satisfaction and good functioning at work and at home with a minimum of role conflict."

Rapoport et al, 2002, define WLB as "Work-personal life integration" suggesting that different aspects of work and life need to be integrated depending upon one's priorities, so that 'balance' need not imply equal amount of personal resources like time and energy. Thus integration of different parts of life independent of the time allocated to them, leads to individuals' satisfaction about their respective lives.

Greenhaus, Collins and Shaw (2003) have found that employees who spent proportionally g more time on family out of total time, showed higher level of quality of life (QoL), than those who spent equal amount of time on both domain, while the ones who spent more time on work, had lowest level of QoL. They thus suggest three key components of WLB: time balance, involvement balance, and satisfaction balance.

Frone, 2003 defines WLB as "Low levels of conflict and high levels of inter-role facilitation represent work-family balance". Greenhaus & Powell, 2006, define work-life balance as "the extent to which an individual's effectiveness and satisfaction in work and family roles are compatible with the individual's life-role priorities at a given point in time". According to Grzywacz & Carlson, 2007, contend that WLB can be considered "as accomplishment of role-related expectations that are negotiated and shared between an individual and his/her role partners in the work and family domains." Whereas according to Voydanoff, 2008, "Work-life balance is the global assessment that work and family resources are sufficient to meet work and family demands such that participation is effective in both domains."

Thus consensus is limited on a formal definition of WLB. Greenhaus et al (2003) stated the major problem in literature as either not mentioning the concept of WLB, or even at places where it's mentioned, then it is further not explicitly defined. Additionally, researchers have measured this construct differently and used different approaches. (Greenhaus et al). Kalliath and Brough (2008) have identified six different definitions that are commonly used within the literature:

1. WLB is reflective of a person's orientation towards different life roles
2. A person's display of degree of control over working conditions like when, where and how they work.
3. Minimal inter-role conflict and higher of inter-role facilitation between work and family domains

4. WLB displays the degree to which an individual is satisfied with his or her work role and family role

5. WLB is about attaining satisfying experiences in all life domains

6. The compatibility between a person's satisfaction in work and family roles and his or her life role priorities at any given point in time

Conceptualization

Work-life balance has been conceptualized differently by different authorities. Guest (2002) defines balance as, "satisfaction and good functioning at work and at home with a minimum of role conflict." Researchers also conceptualize WLB as a three dimensional time and space measure involving personal time, family care, and work (Ungerson & Yeandle, 2005; Williams, 2001). However, some researchers disagree with the concept of WLB as they believe that the term is gender neutral and that does not take into consideration power cultural barriers and hurdles that women face in organizations (Smithson & Stokoe, 2005).

The WLB has been a long researched concept, and was initially researched in response to issues related to work management and family life (Lewis, Gambles, & Rapoport, 2007). The approach, however, has over the time, undergone change. First, WLB was considered a concept important to the problems of working mothers and dual-earner families, later the focus shifted and gradually broadened, to include overall issues of work and family life.

Guest, 2002 discusses a set of independent, intermediate and outcome variables to describe a preliminary model for research and analysis.

ignou   Work –Life Balance among Women Professionals

Nature and consequences of work-life balance (Guest, 2002)

Determinants	Nature of balance	Consequences/ impact
Organizational factors	Subjective indicators	Work satisfaction
Demands of work	Balance-emphasis	Life satisfaction
Culture of work	equally on home and	Mental health/well being
Demands of home	work	Stress/illness
Culture of home	Balance-home central	
Individual factors	Balance- work central	Behavior/ performance
Work orientation	Spillover and /or	at work
Personality	interference of work	Behavior/ performance
Energy	to home	at home
Personal control and	Spillover and /or	Impact on others at work
Coping	interference of home	
Gender	to work	Impact on others at
Age	Objective indicators	Home
Life and career	Hours of work	
stage	"Free" time	
	Family roles	

Independent Variables

Gender

Researchers like Colbeck, 2006, in their study of academic faculty of universities, found a gender difference in the way in which men and women balanced work/family issues. They reported that "male participants spent somewhat more time on work and less time on personal activities than the female participants, but for women, work and family roles were not mutually exclusive." Keeping the problems faced by women, in mind, some organizations have introduced work-life programs to facilitate WLB, especially for women like part time tenure track options for women. (Drago and Williams, 2000; Wolf-Wendel and Ward, 2006). According to Philipsen (2008), social structure can create challenges for women as they "are asked to make choices, furthermore, their male counterparts hardly ever have to make, namely the choice between family and work".

There have also been several qualitative studies of the personal and professional lives of corporate employees, understand how employees experiences balance work with their lives outside of the workplace. Emslie and Hunt (2009) conducted qualitative research through semistructured interviews with men and women in occupations including IT, nursing, engineering, and media. They reported that although maintaining WLB was difficult for men and women but that such issues extended for a longer duration in women as compared to men.

ignou   Work –Life Balance among Women Professionals

Harrington, Van Deusen, and Ladge (2010) also conducted semi-structured interviews with employees and reported that half of their participants found it difficult to juggle work with family. Medved (2004) studied the way in which couples balanced family responsibilities in terms of daily routines, and reported that mothers dealt with more expectations such as childcare and tasks like regular meal preparation. Similar findings were reported by Guendouzi, 2006, who stated that that most of the household responsibilities, including childcare, continued to be performed by mothers.

To cope up with these extra family life expectations, mothers often choose part-time employment in an effort to better manage work-life demands. Warren (2004) studied the impact of WLB and personal finances, and examined how part-time employment affected work/family balance of working mothers, as compared to full time employees. They reported that though, job satisfaction was reportedly similar, mothers working part time were less satisfied with their social lives, and also reported fewer financial resources. Thus part time opportunity may not completely solve the evasive issue of maintaining WLB.

Spencer-Dawe (1999) strain experienced by single working mothers in terms of financial loss, and loss of work time and work place credibility. Additional strain made it harder for them to reach out to supervisors, which resulted in their being called in to cover during staff shortages and the expectation that they would take work home. As a result, the time that they expected to have with family was spent working. However, researchers McCubbin 1995, report that presence of extended family support may help in better adjusting to and coping with stress.

Rosenfield et al, in their gender focused study, found that women were more likely than men to have mental health problems related to having multiple roles. Similar findings were also reported by Emslie et al. (2004), who found that work-home conflict was associated with mental health problems. MacDonald, et al. (2005) found that women experienced more stress about childcare issues. They found that women experienced more stress than men because they spent a greater number of hours doing unpaid household work.

Women's economic role has expanded, changing the dynamics of labor division within families and affecting work life balance (WLB) at the same time. However, while women's entry into job market has increased rapidly, men's entry into housework has been more gradual, thus making WLB a critical public issue policy. Other factors like parenting add to family's work hours, thus influencing work life balance. (Marshal, 2006)

Sector

In earlier times, attaining work-life balance was considered the sole responsibility of the employee, not the employer (Bailyn, 1993). As compared to these historic times, the recent 21st century trend makes it necessary for institutions of higher education to adopt meaningful work life policies. (Bailyn 1993; Gappa et al, 2007 Wiliams, 2000)

Researchers have reinforced the existence of WLB problems for employers in the corporate world. Matos and Galinsky (2011) analyzed data from the National Study of the Changing Workforce and the National Study of Employers, They considered sectors like health services; hospitality, restaurant, and tourism; manufacturing; and retail. They found that the

ignou   Work –Life Balance among Women Professionals

majority of employees, 60-69%,reported that they lacked time for themselves and for their spouses/partners. Researchers also found that employees who were employed in flexible work environments reported that they had greater amounts of time to spend with their spouses/partners and children.

Research by Friedman and Greenhaus (2000) substantiates this finding; they surveyed employed business school alumni from two institutions in an attempt to investigate the relationship between work and home for corporate employees. Respondents, particularly those who were parents, reported a lack of time for family. Those who worked for employers that they identified as family-friendly, however, reported lower levels of conflict between their personal and professional lives. Friedman and Greenhaus concluded that support at home and family friendly workplaces can help to ease work-life integration.

Quantitative and qualitative research has documented that work-life balance is problematic for corporate employees. However, work-life balance research on the corporate workplace, as depicted in the preceding studies, often draws conclusions from studies of employees across different industries.

At the same time, Barnett, 1998 and Zedeck, 1992 found these quantitative bodies of worklife balance researches to be having a amajor drawback, that is, an overreliance on selfreported survey data.

Many researchers like Finkel, Olswang and She 1994; Grant et al, 2000; Harrington and

Ladge, 2009; Ward and Wolf-Wendel, 2005, have reported that many academicians and faculty members fear to work-life policies to save their reputation as a scholar.

While such research offers insight into broad workplace trends, Anderson, Morgan, and Wilson (2002) noted that we know little about the work-life experiences of employees by industry. Varied organizational cultures exist across industries. Thus, employees in different industries may experience different work-life balance problems. These cultures make the validity of extending conclusions from the corporate workplace to the academy questionable (Anderson et al., 2002).

Cultures

A study of 30 European countries (European Commission, 2005) involving work practices and support along with impact on personal domain, showed a wide range of variability among statuary support, leave facilities, childcare services, flexible working arrangements and financial allowances. Countries differed in the degree of their implementation, prioritizing some policies over others. The importance of promoting work-life initiatives on the macro level is linked to the current low fertility rates, resulting in a reversed birth pyramid , lower participation of women in paid employment as a result of lack of childcare facilities and thus, gender pay gaps, among other reasons (OECD, 2007). In these European countries, state support for child care ensures work-life integration according to one's needs and priorities at the micro level, and a higher competitive advantage over other countries at the macro level. (European Commission, 2005; OECD, 2007)

ignou   Work –Life Balance among Women Professionals

Policies and their uptake

In Spain, family plays a strong role in the creation of welfare and distribution of income and services (Moreno, 2004; Salido & Moreno, 2007). Although the state support is limited and mostly based on pensions, and the level of social assistance is low, there is a sense of intra family support and all incoming resources are distributed and shared among family members, resulting in the members enjoying a relatively high level of well-being. With the rise women's educational levels and higher participation in the paid labor, dual income households have emerged (Chinchilla, Poelmans, & León, 2003; Moreno, 2004), which have contributed to this family support system. (Naldini, 2003; Tobia, 2001)

The women from the generation between 40 and 64, have contributed considerably to the current system and family support (Moreno, 2004). This has resulted in a household poverty rate of only 5% compared to an individual poverty rate of 36%. This has resulted in the government directing its expenditures to other welfare programs, beyond household and personal services.

Theoretical framework in WLB research

Work and personal life have been integrated and equated in different ways like work-life balance, work-family conflict, spillover, enrichment etc (Greenhaus & Powell, 2006, clark 2000). Conflict theory, that states that various roles lead to role conflict and stress, has been mostly used to understand the work-family interface (Eby et al., 2005; Greenhaus & Powell,

2006).

Conflict perspective:

Work-family conflict is among the most widely used concepts (Kelly et al., 2008). It is related to the role theory and is defined as "a form of interrole conflict in which the role pressures from work and family domains are mutually incompatible in some respect. That is, participation in the work (family) role is made more difficult by virtue of participation in the family (work) role" (Greenhaus & Beutell, 1985). Although initially the impact of conflict was considered unidimensional, recently it has been thought as a bi-dimensional, that is, work interfering with family and family interfering with work (Frone et al., 1997). Most studies have tended to focus on one dimensional flow, that is, extent of work interference with life (Kelly et al., 2008). In a review of a US large-scale surveys, Bellavia & Frone, 2005 found that between a quarter and half of respondents experienced work-family conflict, while family-work conflict was significantly lower (around 10-14%)

Role conflict has been defined as the "simultaneous occurrence of two or more sets of pressures in the work place such that compliance with one would make compliance more difficult with the other" (Bacharach, Bamberger & Conley, 1991). There are three major forms of work-family conflict and they are: time-based conflict, strain-based conflict and behaviour-based conflict (Greenhaus & Beutell, 1985). Time-based conflict is competition over time spent in different roles, such as work schedules, work orientation, marriage, children and spouse employment patterns may all produce pressures to participate extensively in the work role or the family roles (Gilbreath, 2004). Conflict is experienced

ignou   Work –Life Balance among Women Professionals

when these time pressures are incompatible with the demands of the other role (Williams & Alliger, 1994). Similar to time-based conflict, quantitative role overload is defined as the conflict between organizational demands and the time allocated to the individual by the organization to satisfy those demands (Bacharach, Bamberger & Conley, 1991).

Strain-based conflict are work stressors that can produce strain symptoms such as tension, anxiety, fatigue, depression, apathy and irritability, these symptoms of strain exist when stress in one role affects one's performance in another role (Higgins, Duxbury & Lyons, 2010; Bacharach, Bamberger & Conley, 1991). Behaviour-based conflicts are specific patterns of in-role behaviour that may be incompatible with expectations regarding behaviour in another and if a person is unable to adapt, then they are likely to experience conflict between the roles (Greenhaus & Beutell).

Work/family conflict can best be understood theoretically as a form of stress response to role overload and overlapping or incompatible non-work and work demands (Watkins, 1995). Many employees are taking work home with them, which has blurred the boundary between work and family (Baral & Bhargava, 2010). It has been found that work-specific role stressors serve as predictors of job burnout, job dissatisfaction (Bacharach, Bamberger & Conley, 1991), turnover intentions and physical symptoms (Judge & Colquitt, 2004).

Enrichment Perspective

Enrichment perspective refers to the positive side of work-family interface. Concepts describing positive link between work and life domains are also known as positive spillover,

ignou   Work –Life Balance among Women Professionals

enhancement engagement, work-family enrichment and facilitation (Carlson, Kacmar, Grzywacz & Wayne, 2006; Greenhaus & Powell, 2006). The difference between these concepts is their varying emphasis on received benefits, experiences, and improvement of role performance (Carlson et al). Example, work-family facilitation refers to a positive reinforcement where resources from one role, like skills gained, facilitate involvement in the other role (Wayne, Musica & Fleeson, 2004). Similarly, enhancement refers to the social and psychological resources acquired through participation in various roles, while enrichment refers to the "experiences in one role that can improve the quality of life in the other" (Greenhaus & Powell, 2006) and positive spillover refers to experiences, like moods, skills, values, and behaviors transferred from one role to another (Carlson, et al., 2006).

According to Frone et al, 2003, work-family enrichment and work-family conflict have no correlation and thus should be considered as independent concepts, and they can be experienced parallel since they are different, but are both bi-directional. (Frone, 2003; Grzywacz & Butler, 2005). Thus, according to Frone et al, 2003, low degree of inter-role conflict and high degree of inter-role facilitation leads to work-family balance. Researchers have voiced the importance of establishing a specific definition to enhance research and understanding (Greenhaus et al., 2003; Grzywacz & Carlson, 2007; Kalliath & Brough, 2008). Various authors have defined, classified and studied WLB differently. Carlson and Grzywacz (2008) classify the concept using three perspectives: equality, fit and role performance. The equality perspective views both domains as equal and suggests balancing between the two domains can be done by distributing resources, like attention, time, etc. equally between the two spheres (Greenhaus, Collins, & Shaw, 2003). According to the fit perspective, the balance does not only reflect the resource investment made by a person but also satisfaction derived by the individual. Here resource investment in a role is done according to one's values, while this investment is evaluated through an individual's self assessment of his role performance across a variety of domains (Sheldon & Niemiec, 2006). According to the role performance perspective, an individual reaches work-life balance by negotiating on expectations with both the work and family. Thus this perspective emphasizes on the social basis of work-life balance (Grzywacz & Carlson, 2007).

Border theory

Clark (2000) defines balance as satisfaction and good functioning at work and at home, with a minimum of role conflict. The researcher also describes domain negotiation as a dynamic process influenced by the similarities and differences between the work and non-work domains of an individual's life. Clark (2000) has considered work and home as two distinct spheres-like two countries, each with its own culture, and has included several kinds of borders, like physical borders such as the walls of one's workspace, temporal borders such as one's work schedule, and the psychological borders that dictate when one's thoughts, behaviors, and emotions are suitable in one domain and not the other. According to Clark movement between the domains can be likened to border crossing and often requires individuals to alter their goals and interpersonal styles to meet the demands of each of these settings. Like border crossing, an individual while transitioning from work to other domains, is also affected by the nature of the border. Clark (2000) has described the nature of borders in terms of permeability, flexibility, and blending. Thus, the more the permeability of the border, the more easily positive or negative aspects from other domains can enter, such as

ignou   Work –Life Balance among Women Professionals

spillover of emotions from one sphere to another. Flexibility refers to the degree to which a border will shrink or expand, depending upon the demands of one domain or another. Clark suggested that the more flexible the border, the more freedom an individual has to move between borders, and easier it is for ideas, insights, and emotions to flow more between domains. Additionally, permeability and flexibility around a border leads to blending. This in turn leads to the formation of a *borderland that* cannot be exclusively referred to as either the work or family domain, and within which the individual fulfils both work and family roles, like a family-run business.

Further, according to Clark (2000), in strong/ weak borders, if there exists a similarity in work and home areas then work-family balance can be achieved through weak barriers. But when work and home areas are different, then WLB can be attained though stronger borders. According to Lirio, Lee, Williams, Haugen, and Kossek (2008), supervisors play a critical role in determining whether employees actually take advantage of options designed to support work-family balance. Thus workers who are most comfortable with their colleagues and feel a sense of belonging would be more inclined to request and utilize these programs. The main assumption of border theory is that work and family are separate areas that continue to influence each other, and that individuals continuously negotiate between these two domains in a struggle to attain WLB at every step. The central proposition of border theory is that "integrating work and family facilitates transitions between these domains" (Desrochers & Sargent, 2004)

Many spillover researchers have also examined the emotional influences that work has on employees' home lives and vice versa and have identified important determinants of these influences. However, spillover theory has limitations in that it is based on the existing work society structure and the corresponding assumptions that a "good and normal" employee must spend long hours at work and consider her or his work a priority. Compared to spillover theorists, border theorists assume that working people should spend their time at work and at home somewhat equally, and therefore they argue that "people are daily border-crossers." As a result, employees do not have to try to fit themselves into rigid conceptions of work and family structures. Instead, they may decide how to make or utilize these structures to attain work-life balance with a desired level of flexibility.

Five main models have been used to explain the relationship between work and life. The segmentation model categorizes work and non-work as two separate entities, are lived separately and do not influence each other. The spillover model indicates work and nonwork as entities which can influence each other positively or negatively. Third is the compensation model according to which demands or satisfaction lacking in one domain can be made up in another. Fourth model is the instrumental model that hypothesizes that activities in one sphere can facilitate success in other sphere. Fifth model is the conflict model which suggests that with high level of demands in all domains, conflicts may occur. (Zedeck and Mosier, 1990), (O'Driscoll, 1996). Recent research, especially in dual career families, has focused on the conflict model.

Dimensions

Clark (2001), measured work-life integration in terms of 5 aspects (role conflict, work satisfaction, home satisfaction, family functioning, employee citizenship). Work culture was conceptualized in terms of temporal flexibility, operational flexibility and supportive supervision.

Measuring WLB has been a challenge, due to lack of objectivity in defining balance/ imbalance, and quantifying the degree of balance or imbalance. While social theorists justify measuring working hours as one of the variables defining WLB, other variables remain unclear. It is also unclear how free time is affected by technological progression. While Keynes and Mill suggested technological progression would eventually create more free time for workers, recently Schor et al have suggested that organizations maximize profit by loading employees with more work, thus present generations have more financial resources but less free time than previous generations. The authors suggested measuring work hours, unpaid work hours, and discretionary time in order to determine WLB. (Fisher, 2002)

According to Greenhaus & Beutell (1985) there are three types of work-family conflict: time based, strain-based and behaviour-based conflicts. According to Parasuraman & Greenhaus, 1997, time based conflict occurs "when the time demands of one role make it difficult or impossible to participate in another role". For example, an urgent requirement at the job may coincide with a family function, resulting in the employee having to skip the latter. Strain based conflict occurs "when psychological from the demands of work or family role impacts the other role, making it difficult to fulfil the responsibilities of that role". For example, a person trying to meet sudden or heightened job related requirements, may be strained and may have to skip or delay responding to family needs. Finally, behaviour-based conflict occurs "when the behaviours that are expected or appropriate in the family role are viewed as inappropriate or dysfunctional when used in the work role". For example, a sense of emotional expressiveness in the family role may be misunderstood in the work role, and hence may require behavior modulation leading to stress. Thus, according to Carlson et al., 2000, the concept of work-family conflict includes three-dimensions, that is, time, strain and behavior, and two directions, that is, work-family, family-work.

Organizational factors

Role of supervisor

Managerial support is essential in successfully integrating work-life domains (Anderson et al., 2002; Poelmans & Beham, 2008; Thompson et al., 2004). Thomas & Ganster (1995) proposed that a family-supportive work environment consists of two main elements: family supportive policies and family supportive supervisors. It was found that supervisor support affected employees' perception of the organization as family supportive and consequently decreased work-family conflict (Allen, 2001), while lack of managerial support was closely linked with the experienced work-family conflict (Anderson et al., 2002) and employees' benefit utilization (Thompson et al., 1999). If employees perceive that their organization or supervisor do not encourage benefit use, they will be less likely to use it fearing repercussions for their career (De Cieri, Holmes, Abbot, & Pettit, 2005; Thompson et al., 1999).

Consequently, employees with powerful supervisors are more prone to use work-family policies as they expect their managers to buffer potentially negative career consequences (Blair-Loy & Wharton, 2002).

Work Characteristics

The organizational environment includes the interaction between workers, risk-taking orientation, and a trusting and caring atmosphere; while the structure determines levels of responsibility, decision-making authority and formal reporting relations (Chong & Ma, 2010). Work domain determinants such as job autonomy, schedule flexibility, hours worked, the amount of social support provided by supervisors and coworkers, and the existence of family-friendly work policies directly influence work-life balance (Jennings & McDougald, 2007). Innstrantd, Langballe and Falkum (2010) report that individuals working in occupations that require substantial interaction with others, additional work roles, or professional responsibility for others, are more likely to experience greater numbers of work life balance issues. Additionally, individuals working in a managerial or higher status occupation report higher levels of conflict between work and their personal life. Other factors like concerns about fairness can also affect the attitudes and behaviours of employees and affect their ability to cope with work demands (Judge and Colquitt, 2004).

Colley (2010) and Poelmans, Patel and Beham (2008) in their good amount of qualitative research evidence along with some survey based research evidence, have shown that the mere existence of work-life policies in the academic field is not enough to ensure their utilization or their success.

ignou   Work –Life Balance among Women Professionals

Work Demands:

New technologies and working practices with greater flexibility have been
adopted by several organizations to cater to market competition pressures. (Haworth &
Lewis, 2005). Additional work hours subtract from home time, while high work intensity or
work pressure may result in fatigue, anxiety or other adverse psycho-physiological
consequences that can influence the quality of home and family life (White, et al., 2003).
Even Gappa et al (2007), Mason and Ekman (2007) noticed that fear and stigma can
sometimes surround work-life policies. Because of the ideal worker model, employees often
are concerned that use of work-life policies will damage their professional reputation; they
worry that they will be perceived as less committed to the institution. (Hewlett, 2007;
Thompson 2008, Williams, 2000)

Several studies have examined the advantages of performing multiple roles (Barnett &
Hyde, 2001; Friedman & Greenhaus, 2000; Greenhaus and Powell, 2006; Lee & Phillips 2006;
Sieber 1974). But Gappa, Austin, and Trice (2007) and Williams (2000) concluded that men
are dissatisfied with the ideal worker model

Autonomy:

Individuals with lower levels of perceived control, either due to increased
absence rates or mental health issues, over their work are more likely to report high role
overload and high interference between work and family roles (Baral and Bhargava, 2010;
Hall and Richter, 1988; Jennings and McDougald, Bond and Bunce, 2001). It has also been

explained that providing employees with control over their work serves to improve stress related outcomes, such as lowered anxiety levels, psychological distress, burnout, irritability, psychosomatic health complaints, and alcohol consumption (Bond and Bunce, 2001).

Technology:

Technology can both help and hinder work-life balance. Improvements to technology has helped employers make progress to how business is done, help is more accessible to clients, processes are often more efficient and employees are often more reachable. However, improvements to technology have also made working twenty-four hours a day, seven days a week more accessible to employees (Maxwell & McDougall, 2004). This change has lead to employees working more outside regular office hours, leading to increased interference with employee's home life. Individuals are expected to take whatever time is required to get the job done resulting in them being always the job (Seron & Ferris, 1995).

Constraints

Haworth and Lewis (2005) contend that many work-life issues are the result of structural and social constraints. Godbey, Crawford and Shen (2010) explain that there are three types of constraints: structural, intrapersonal and interpersonal. Structural constraints are external constraints related to the availability of resources required to participate in activities (Alexandris, Tsorbatzoudis & Grouios, 2002). Intrapersonal constraints are primarily concerned with subjective perceptions or assessments of appropriateness and relevance of participation in a given activity by the individual in question (Godbey, Crawford & Shen). The bases for determining such appropriateness and relevance may be

ignou   Work –Life Balance among Women Professionals

psychological, cultural and/or the result of genetic predisposition (Godbey, Crawford & Shen). Interpersonal constraints must be operationalized within a specific culture, in one culture, religion may play a central role in determining who one can participate in an activity, in another, it may play no role (Godbey, Crawford & Shen).

Successful negotiation of these constraints must be conducted in a sequential manner (Godbey, Crawford & Shen, 2010). An individual's attributes, interests, related knowledge and skills, access to facilities, social connectivity, and cultural background, to name a few, are deciding factors in the level of constraints experienced.(Godbey, Crawford & Shen). It could be argued that some types of constraints might influence motivation, which can influence participation (Alexandris, Tsorbatzoudis & Grouios, 2002).

Competition:

Competition relates to the nature and extent of forces that are threatening to the success of an organization. While competition is often considered in positive terms, it can also make working life more difficult (Bloom & Reenen, 2006). Competition can be negative because it can create high-performance practices that lead to negative spillover (White, et al., 2003). In an organization with high turnover, the excess burden is often put on remaining employees (Porter & Alman, 2010).

In addition, many researchers have pointed out that supervisors' support in organizations is very important for balancing work-life demands (Behson, 2005; Mennino et al., 2005; Secret & Sprang, 2001). In particular, supportive supervision allows for rules to be flexible in the

ignou   Work –Life Balance among Women Professionals

case of a family crisis or illness (Clark, 2000). Mennino et al.'s (2005) study also used the same variables as the present quantitative study to measure supervisory support. Based on their positive results, it is expected that supervisory support will also be positively related to work-life balance in the present study. Secret and Sprang (2001) conducted a study with a sub-sample of 374 employed parents that was representative of employees at small and medium companies. The findings revealed positive effects of informal supervisory support on work-family balance. The authors pointed out that studies using are necessary because they can strengthen the construct validity of the findings.

A culture of honesty and trust between staff and management facilitate WLB programs. (Maxwell & McDougall, 2004). Some benefits with work life balance programs at the organizational level include: lower recruitment, lower training costs, improved productivity (Ulshafer, Potgeisser & Lima, 2005), decreased job burnout (Haar & Roche, 2010), easier service delivery, enhanced quality service, enhanced employee capability, less absence, lower turnover, employee flexibility, skills to succeed in rapidly changing markets (Maxwell & McDougall, 2004), increased organizational commitment, increased levels of organizational citizenship behaviours (Baral & Bhargava, 2010) and increased levels of participation within the organization and initiative (Haar & Roche, 2010). It has been found that work-life balance programs allowed supervisors the option to help staff and made the management role less difficult (Maxwell & McDougall, 2004).

All of the positive emotions that employees experience by reducing their stress levels are associated with an outward focus of attention, such that when people are happy, they report

ignou   Work –Life Balance among Women Professionals

increased liking for others and are more willing to initiate conversations and offer help (Rothbard, 2001). It has been reported that the lure of work life balance programs may not be in the utilization, but in the access to them (Porter & Alman, 2010). Porter and Alman found that employees who believe that they have sufficient flexibility in when, what, and where work is completed, regardless of if they participate in alternative work schedules, are those most greatly affected. When an individual leads a balanced life, they are likely to experience vigor as a component of work engagement (Cinamon & Rich, 2010). Vigor has been characterized as comprising high levels of effort, energy, resilience and persistence (Cinamon & Rich). Involvement in multiple individual roles can result in benefits both to the individual and the organization (Ruderman, Ohlott, Panzer & King, 2002), therefore, it is important for employers to recognize these benefits and support employees commitments outside of the job by being flexible and providing them the opportunity to engage in these activities.

Job status is also an important factor regarding work-life balance. Many employees, especially women, choose to work part time because they believe that it is likely to make it easier to balance work-family demands, even though part-time work tends to be less wellpaid and less secure than full-time work (Evans, 2002). Additionally, certain part-time schedules, such as weekend shifts, make it easier for mothers to take care of their young children during weekdays (Garey, 1999). In particular, Guest (2002, p. 266) pointed out that the work context, such as demands of work, affect perceptions of work-life balance "that can be defined subjectively or objectively." For example, full-time employees have more work demands than part-time workers, so they are likely to face more work-life conflict (Chung, Garfield, Elliott, Carey, Eriksson, & Schuster, 2007).

ignou   Work –Life Balance among Women Professionals

Individual factors

Work and family are closely interconnected domains of human life (Edwards & Rothbard, 2000) and meeting the demands from both work and family can be very challenging and can lead to issues with work-life balance (Md-Sidin, et al., 2008).

Gender is a topic that has been extensively reviewed within the work life balance literature. Warren (2004) explained that women with domestic responsibilities have taken on part-time jobs as a beneficial way to maintain their labour market skills, as a secondary source of income and sustain interest outside of the home. However, there is also resulting conflict between their work and family commitments and responsibilities (Drew, 2005). Porter & Ayman, 2010 argue that the reason for this is that women typically assume the majority of childbearing duties. This responsibility can influence both role stress and negative attitudes at work (e.g. role conflict, job burnout and dissatisfaction) and are positively associated with disruptions at home (Bacharach, Bamberger & Conley, 1991).

Many researchers (Haworth & Lewis, 2005; Jennings & McDougald, 2007) report that men and women tend to prioritize work and family roles differently; men typically sacrifice more at home and women tend to sacrifice more at work for home commitments. It has been found that women's level of involvement at work did not differ from men's, however they did admit to a certain level of concern with home issues at work (Hall & Richter, 1988). Martins, Eddleston and Veiga (2002) found that women's career satisfaction was negatively affected by work-family conflict throughout their lives whereas men showed adverse effects only later

ignou   Work –Life Balance among Women Professionals

in their career.

Marital status

Martins, Eddleston & Veiga, (2002) found married individuals to give more
emphasis to their personal lives than their single counterparts. The reason could be the former
experiencing a lack of separation or difficulty keeping separation between work and home
boundaries (Hall & Richter, 1988), which can negatively influence both work and family life.
Md-Sidin, et al. (2008) reported that individuals who are married experience more work-life
conflict than those who are unmarried. Though most research has focused on the demands of
work and its role in causing the conflict, there has been a recent focus towards role of life outside
work, including a body of research focusing the impact of various types of family commitments.
Mauno and Kinnunen, 1999, report a finninsh study of 215 dual earning couples exploring the
impact of range of work stressors on marital satisfaction. They found that most of the stressors
affected marital satisfaction due to job exhaustion and its impact on psychosomatic health.
Among the stressors, work family conflict and time pressure had major impact. However, there
was no marital spillover from one partner to another. In another study, Vinokur et al, 1999,
evaluated the effect of both work and family stressors on the mental health and functioning of
women in US air force. They found that high involvement in both family and work affected the
outcome. Job, marital distress, and work-family conflict adversely impacted mental health

Parental Status

ignou   Work –Life Balance among Women Professionals

The presence or absence of children in the family continues to make a significant difference in the degree of balance that individuals experience (Tausig & Fenwick, 2001). Parental status has been found to be a determinant of parents placing increased importance on the role of family (Blau, et al., 1998). Family responsibilities such as household time demands, family responsibility level, household income, spousal support and life course stage have been found to be sources of work-life stress (Jennings & McDougald, 2007).

Dual earner couples with no children report greater work-life balance, while both single and married parents report significantly lower levels of perceived balance compared to single, non-parents (Tausig & Fenwick).

Age and Lifecycle

Wang, Lawler & Shi, (2010) found that age and lifecycle determine and influence work life stress experienced by individuals. Recent generations have experienced a change in lifestyle preferences leading to nomenclatural divisions. Those born after 1969, or the so called "Generation X", are said to prefer a lifestyle that includes non-work time, irrespective of other responsibilities, hence may actively seek employers who offer work-life balance arrangements (Maxwell, 2005). Tausig and Fenwick (2001) reported that older adults report greater success with work-life balance.

Personality

Jennings and McDougald (2007) found that certain personality differences

ignou   Work –Life Balance among Women Professionals

predispose individuals to work-life balance issues. The tendency to feel guilty, to be loyal towards others, a lack of sensitivity towards others and the need and desire for "being there" for family members and being unable to manage a new situation has been suggested to influence the level to which an individual experiences work life balance issues (Bekker, et al., 2010). A person's emotional response to a role is a critical factor influencing their interpersonal availability and psychological presence in a different role (Rothbard, 2001). Individuals with high negative affectivity seem to experience more negative interaction between work and family (Bekker et al.).

These individuals who lay emphasis on developing and actualizing their inner potential, and satisfy their basic psychological needs to attain autonomy, competence and relatedness,are labeled as intrinsically oriented individuals. Thus, pursuing intrinsic life value orientations is positively correlated with well-being and optimal functioning (Van den Broeck, Vansteenkiste & Has De Witte, 2010). On the other hand, extrinsically oriented individuals adopt an outward oriented focus and try to impress others by acquiring external signs of worth importance. Thus, holding an extrinsic work value orientation as an employee can be associated with lower job satisfaction, job vitality, and job commitment and higher exhaustion (Van den Broeck, Vansteenkiste & Has De Witte, 2010).

Challenges to balance

The difficulties of balancing between work and family have become one of the issues among the scholars. In order to balance work and family life, women and men have developed ways to navigate the spheres of work and family. As Hertz's (1986) study revealed, contemporary

ignou   Work –Life Balance among Women Professionals

dual-earner couples have challenges different from the traditional ideal marriage. "Work and its rewards still shape a couple's life chances; but instead of being a single career or job defining marital roles, there are two careers, qualifying each spouse as a breadwinner"

Changing times/current scenario

Changing times: Winslow (2005) analyzed data from a sample of respondents from the Quality of Employment Survey and the 1997 National Study of the Changing Workforce survey. All of the respondents whose data were included in Winslow's analysis were between the ages of 18 and 65 and were married or the parent of a child younger than age 18.

Work family conflict was measured by the question, "How much would you say your job and your family life interfere with each other?" Winslow (2005) found that the mean level of reported work-life conflict was higher in 1997 than in 1977. Conflict was most acute for respondents who were parents. While quantitative studies like those by Matos and Galinsky (2011).

Friedman and Greenhaus (2000), and Winslow (2005) are useful in that they affirm the existence of work-life balance problems for employees in the corporate world, they provide little information regarding how employees experience work-life balance or what types of specific problems they face. The quantitative body of work-life balance research has been criticized for an overreliance on self-reported survey data (Barnett, 1998; Zedeck, 1992). Quantitative data do not reveal the ways in which individuals "understand and negotiate the intersections between work and home life" (Emslie & Hunt, 2009, p. 154). Further, some quantitative studies, like Winslow's, continue to measure the relationship between respondents' personal and professional lives as a single construct despite the fact that research has shown that the relationship is multidimensional (Greenhaus & Beutell, 1985).

Current scenario: White, et al. (2003) have reported employees are spending more time than ever before at their jobs; resulting in them working the equivalent of an extra month per annum. Being overworked can lead to work-life conflict, because of the pressures from work and family domains being mutually incompatible (Bacharach, Bamberger & Conley, 1991). Such conditions suggest concerns over well-being and work life balance issues (Jennings & McDougald, 2007). It may come as no surprise that many workers are questioning the amount of time and energy devoted to work. (Maxwell & McDougall, 2004). Many now value the idea of work-life balance and see it as a criterion of success (Jennings & McDougald).

Strategies for WLB

Individual strategies for WLB

Even though there are various mechanisms at the organizational level, individuals at their own level, try to reduce work life conflict outcomes to a certain extent by using their own resources to attain WLB. Various boundary management and coping strategies are used.

Boundary Management

According to the boundary theory, individuals construct, manage and negotiate worknon/

ignou   Work –Life Balance among Women Professionals

work boundaries to make their environment simpler and extract sense out of it (Ashforth, Kreiner, & Fugate, 2000). Research has identified three types of boundaries: spatial, temporal and psychological. Additionally, there are tangible boundaries that divide the time, place and people from the work and personal environments, suggested by the work-family border theory (Clark, 2000). The level of flexibility and permeability of boundaries, that is their possibility to shrink or expand and enter another domain, affects individuals' perceptions (Nippert-Eng, 1996). Flexible and permeable boundaries are considered to be weak and therefore lead to a situation of "integration". While impermeable and inflexible boundaries lead to a situation of "segmentation" (Ashforth et al., 2000; Clark, 2000; Nippert-Eng, 1996).

Boundary management refers to how mental boundaries are enacted through the daily activities aimed at either separating or integrating the different domains (Nippet-Eng, 1996), taking into consideration how these boundaries are crossed, maintained or changed over a period of time (Ashforth, Kreiner, & Fugate, 2000). Individuals indulge in boundary management by using these three ways- proactive way (by forecasting the situation that can produce conflict), active way (by processing boundary work simultaneously), and reactive way (by rationalizing the choices being made previously) (Ashforth et al., 2000; Kreiner & Fugate, 2000). According to Kossek, Noe and DeMarr (1999), boundary management strategy is defined as set of principles by which individuals approach work and life demands and expectations, that is, by separating or integrating boundaries.

A study of French managers by Languilaire et al, 2009, found that most respondents

ignou   Work –Life Balance among Women Professionals

reported a tendency for segmentation most of the times, as part of their proactive strategy for most successful management of the work-non-work spheres, and prevention of their mutual negative effects. However, at various points in time, managers reported a tendency of integration of various spheres of life, as part of their reactive strategy, to find a short term solution for newer work- life issues. Therefore, segmentation seemed to be a proactive approach whereas integration was a reactive approach, being a more spontaneous way of boundary role management that did not require planning or arrangements.

The study of professionals' use of telecommuting using telework options showed that employees using integration boundary managers experience higher level of family to work spillover (Kossek, et al, 2006), in line with the conceptualization of Ashfroth et al. (2000). Contrary to popular belief, those employees who integrate various sides of life might experience more conflict due to the need of switching back and forth from one domain to another. Thus, if something negative occurs in one domain it would tend to spill easier on the other domain and might not be buffered by the accumulated positive events in various life spheres (Kossek et al., 2006). Therefore, the best predictors of individuals' well-being was perceived job control over where, when and how the work was done and the segmentation boundary management strategy. In line with this finding, Clark (2002) uncovered that high flexibility and low permeability of boundaries were associated with the lowest levels of work- family conflict. However, context is important here because first, individual preferences are crucial and affect the choice of the enacted boundaries and consequent work-family assessment (Rau & Hyland, 2002); and second boundary management is also affected by socio-cultural constraints arising out of work and non-work demands (Languilaire, 2007). Thus, context needs to be understood in totality, for a more complete understanding of the phenomenon.

Coping refers to cognitive and behavioral efforts used by the person to deal with situations where the demands exceed the available resources (Lazarus & Folkman, 1984). Lazarus and Folkman (1984) stated that there are two types of coping strategies that exist-emotion focused and problem focused. The first step is to face a problem, and once that situation is perceived as a problem, in the next step, this person analyses if the problem is posing any kind of threat to his/her well-being (primary appraisal). If yes, then as a further step, person assesses the ways of coping with this problem (secondary appraisal). At this stage of secondary appraisal, person chooses the coping strategy as either problem focused or emotion focused. If a problem focused approach is decided to be followed, then the person clearly defines the problem and resolves it, or may also adapt the interpretation of that situation. Most researchers consider problem-solving strategy to be more effective as the person feels more in control of the situation (Kirschmeyer, 1993; Rotondo, Carlson, & Kincaid, 2003).

However, when individuals have little possibility to change this situation the emotion-focused coping is preferred (Bhagat, Allie & Ford, 1995). According to Hall (1972) there are three types of strategies. Type 1 coping refers to the structural role definition, when structurally imposed expectations of others are altered, like alteration of work timings. Type 2 refers to personal redefinition of the external role demands or re-prioritization. Type 3 -role of reactive behavior-refers to individual attempts to satisfy everyone's expectations. Instead of targeting the conflict or the related perceptions, the person tries to put more efforts to reach all objectives. Research suggests that the latter strategy is the least efficient as it does not solve the core problem and might only increase the level of stress (Kirschmeyer, 1993).

Different coping strategies yield different results. Research has shown that passive coping, like denial or disengagement, was related to higher levels of work-family conflict of all kinds, while this was not the case of active coping (Andreassi, 2006). Also, problem-solving coping was negatively related to strain-based family-work conflict, but not with strain and time-based work-family conflict (Lapierre & Allen, 2006). Besides, positive thinking was found to have a good positive correlation with WLB, as coping with a problem using positive thinking increases work-family and family-work facilitation. (Rotondo, Carlson, & Kincaid, 2003). Thompson, Poelmans, Allen, & Andreassi (2007) extended the Lazarus and Folkman (1984) model and developed a conceptual model that brings together different approaches to coping, reviewing personal and situational antecedents to coping specifically with work-family conflict. They suggest that when faced with a conflict between these areas, the individual passes through a three-stage process. First, the conflict is evaluated in terms of whether it is a threat or not. Second, the situation is assessed in terms of possible actions. Third, a specific method is chosen to deal with the situation. Regarding the possible strategies, various classifications of coping strategies were suggested. Behson (2002) proposed different types of coping strategies based on different behaviors, and concluded that the use of these strategies lead to a decreased experience of family-to-work conflict and stress, as long as there is a supportive organizational environment. Thus context is important in coping.

Drach-Zahavy and Somech (2008) for the first time gave a bidirectional concept of coping strategies, in which eight categories of behavioral strategies can be used by individuals to resolve conflict. These strategies are organized by the degree of expectation the individual has regarding the performance at home or at work.

Thus, the choice of coping strategies is also dependent on the individual's context that affects the choice of strategy the person will use to cope with work- life conflict. Factors that influence this choice are organizational support or the support of the organizational culture, level of control that a person has about a particular fact, and job characteristics of the employee (Thompson et al., 1999; Allen, 2001)

Outcomes of WLB

According to Greenhaus and Powell (2006), participation in multiple roles leads to three positive outcomes. First, positive effects may be added, like feeling of gratification in both work and family, leading to feelings of happiness and quality of life. Second, negative influences like strain may get buffered. Third, there may be a transfer of positive experiences between domains. Thus involvement in multiple roles across different domains can result in positive outcomes related to work and life, while buffering the negative experiences at the same time.

There has been an increased focus on balancing multiple life roles and managing the boundary between work and family. With the increasing focus and pressure to balance all of

ignou   Work –Life Balance among Women Professionals

these different life domains, there has been increasing levels of burnout reported by employees (Bacharach, Bamberger & Conley, 1991). Work life balance issues have been found to affect one"s identity, well-being and quality of functioning (Cinamon & Rich, 2010).

Diminished organizational commitment, job satisfaction, life satisfaction, and increased stress and turnover intentions are certainoutcomes of lack of WLB (Major & Lauzun, 2010). Ashforth, Kreiner & Fugate (2000) caution that blurring the line between work and personal life by bringing day care, recreation facilities and other aspects of personal life to work it makes it more difficult for employees to transition between roles and may compromise the integrity of home, work and third places (Hall & Richter, 1988). In trying to find a solution to a major problem that employees are facing, it is possible that it has created another problem. Research has demonstrated that work interference with family is more prevalent than family interference with work and is more likely to be influenced by workplace factors and supportive supervisor behaviours (Major & Lauzun, 2010).

Job involvement and family support

Job involvement has been described as "psychological identification with a job" (Kanungo, 1982). Researchers like Reitz and Jewell (1979) defined job involvement as the"importance of work in an individual's daily life." Organizational effectiveness and productivity can be affected by Job involvement, making it an important attitudinal variable that impacts work (Seo,2013). Organizations may be significantly benefited by employees showing

ignou   Work –Life Balance among Women Professionals

high levels of job involvement (Diefendorff, 2002). Thus, Job involvement may be linked with or affect work performance, efficiency and behavior (Yang, 2006)

Organizational commitment correlates with job involvement. This may be because committed employees have a sense of belonging towards their organization leading them to perceive their jobs as vital to their organizational membership, and involvement with the job as an indicator of their loyalty towards their organization (Chughtai, 2008; Ng Thomas et al, 2015). Employees with high levels of job involvement tend to significantly benefit the organization (Diefendorff et al., 2002), and are also likely to have high job satisfaction and commitment to their careers and their organizations (Ng Thomas et al, 2015).

Additionally, employees who are more job involved are likely to believe in the compatibility of personal and organizational goals. This makes them tend to focus on job activities even in their spare time like thinking of ways to perform even better (Tastan, 2013). They are likely to feel view themselves as competent and successful, and may be inclined to assist others at work, and contribute to innovation in the organization (Tastan, 2013). Research has also shown that higher job involvement may correlate positively with job performance, lack of absenteeism, turnover, success, and organizational commitment (Kanungo, 1982b). Additionally, researchers have shown a positive relationship between job involvement and innovative behaviors. For these reasons, employee job involvement has become a major research subject in several related research fields. (Tastan, 2013, Dimitriades, 2007, Mudrak, 2004).

The definition of job involvement has changed, evolved and been conceptualized in different ways, probably due to complexity of the construct (Robbins, 2013). While Blau and Boal's (1987) approach focused on psychological identification, Robbins' (2013) approach is somewhat similar to Blau and Boal's (1987). According to them, "a job-involved person considers work as an important part of his or her psychological life." Paullay and colleagues (1994) have defined the concept of job involvement as the "degree to which individuals are cognitively preoccupied with, engaged in, and concerned with their present job."

Among these various conceptualizations, Kanungo's (1982) definition was adopted for this study. Kanungo described job involvement as a "generalized cognitive state of psychological identification with the individual's cognition about his or her identification with work and strong support of the self-image definition of job involvement."

Effects of demographic variables on job involvement have been studied, and researchers have reported inconsistent findings. According to some researchers (Morrow et al., 1988), male employees showed higher levels of job involvement than females. Whereas other researchers like Blau & Boat, 1989, reported no correlation between gender and job involvement.

Uygur et al, 2009, have grouped Job involvement into four perspectives. These are: 1) work as a central life interest, 2) active participation in the job, 3) performance as central to self-esteem, and 4) performance compatible with self-concept. In work as a central life interest, a person considers job involvement as the degree to which the work situation is important and central to his/her identity as it gives the worker an opportunity to satisfy main needs. In the second category, that is, active participation in the job, high job involvement is seen as an opportunity to take job decisions, contributing to company goals, and eventually to self-determination. In performance related perspectives, job involvement is seen as coinciding with performance in work place, which is perceived as necessary for self-esteem and self-concept.

Some researchers report that since Job involvement influences the amount of energy and time invested on work, it may lead to conflict between work and family roles (Frone et al., 1992). Greenhaus et al. (1989) reported that job involvement increased the work-family conflict along the time-based and strain–based dimensions among women. According to them, the reason for this was the requirement of high levels of psychological involvement which in turn led to increased energy and time being devoted to job, resulting in WFC. Thus, job involvement is reported to be positively correlated with time commitment to work and negatively correlated to time commitment to family.

Social support can include family and work place support especially managerial support. Managerial support has been reported to play an important role in organizational effectiveness. Managers are seen by employees, as representatives of the organization who evaluate their performance and report to higher level management. Due to this perception, employees see the support from their managers as organizational support. (Eisenberger, 2002).

Family support has been less discussed in research area on job involvement, and has two components, that is, instrumental support, which refers to tangible help from the partner in the form of participation in home maintenance and child care; and information or emotional support, which refers to information, advice, affirmation of affection, and concern for the receiver's welfare displayed by the partner (Parasuraman & Greenhaus, 1994).

According to Parasuraman, 1996, high levels of instrumental support provided by one's partner can ease the burden of family-role demands, and lead to lesser family-work conflict. They also report positive correlation between spouse support and time spent with family, perhaps due to reciprocity. However, it is not clear if spouse support can affect job involvement especially in women employees in organized sector.

Summary

Supportive work-family culture enhances the psychological resource base for employees by increasing a sense of self-acceptance and flexibility which can aid individuals develop positive affect towards work (Baral & Bhargava). Attaining work-life balance can lead to increased feelings of self efficacy, which is a person's belief about whether they can successfully perform a task (Jex & Gudanowski, 1992).

Work-family enrichment is the extent to which experience in one role improves the quality of life namely performance or affect, in the other role (Baral & Bhargava, 2010). Also, if an employee can better manage their time in one domain, the spillover of demands to another domain is decreased, thus increasing total efficiency (Porter & Alman, 2010). This may suggest that when people are happier with their work role and family life, they will be more likely to help others and to be more enjoyable to work with. It is possible for positive spillover to occur where an employee could utilize skills used in the workplace, such as setting agendas, collecting feedback, directing and counselling – with a few modifications, in the home (DeLong, 1992). Some other benefits that both the employee and employer may experience include: improved productivity, motivation and commitment to the organization (Maxwell & McDougall, 2004).

CHAPTER- 3
RESEARCH METHODOLOGY

RESEARCH METHODOLOGY

Need for the Study

Work/life balance is gaining importance and has become a major issue in India. There are hardly any studies in India focusing on all 3 dimensions and both directions, and their relationship to job involvement and family support. This study not only aims to address this gap, but attempts to dig deeper and capture differences, if any, across sectors, and affect of demographic variables like age, experience, children etc, on WLB and its relationship with job involvement and family support. Job involvement influences an individual's work life, while family support influences family life. Previous research work has established greater instrumental family support may increase job involvement. However, job involvement and family support's interplay in increasing or decreasing WLB along its 3 dimensions, is not clearly established. Additionally there are negligible studies in India studying the impact of job involvement and family support on women professionals

Objectives

The proposed study will be conducted to investigate:

1. To identify the differences between perceived work life balance along each of the individual dimensions of the three dimension, two dimension, and six dimension models of WLB

2. To identify the relationship between years of experience and WLB along each of the individual dimensions of the three dimension, two dimension, and six dimension models of WLB

3. To identify the relationship between age group and WLB along each of the individual dimensions of the three dimension, two dimension, and six dimension models of WLB

4. To identify the differences due to marital status in WLB along each of the individual dimensions of the three dimension, two dimension, and six dimension models of WLB

5. To identify the differences due to presence of children in WLB along each of the individual dimensions of the three dimension, two dimension, and six dimension models of WLB

6. To identify the relationship between family support or type of family support received by the respondents and WLB along each of the individual dimensions of the three dimension, two dimension, and six dimension models of WLB

7. To identify the relationship between job involvement of the respondents and WLB along each of the individual dimensions of the three dimension, two dimension, and six dimension models of WLB

ignou   Work –Life Balance among Women Professionals

8. To identify the relationship between type of sector of the respondents and WLB along each of the individual dimensions of the three dimension, two dimension, and six dimension models of WLB

Study Design

Type of Study:

There are various kinds of researches, for example, Descriptive (e.g., case-study, naturalistic observation, survey), Co relational (e.g., case-control study, observational study), Semi-experimental (e.g., field experiment, quasi-experiment), Experimental (experiment with srandom assignment), Review (literature review, systematic review) and Meta-analytic (meta-analysis) studies.

The present research focuses on the current status of work-life balance and effect of independent variables which were derived from past personal and professional status of respondents, such as type of sector, demographics, job involvement and family support. *Hence, current research work was ex-post facto research.*

Pilot study was carried out before main research, to help in hypothesis generation, and fine tune the main research.

Sources of Data

The researcher approached women professionals across three sectors- healthcare, academic, and corporate services; both public and private, coming from various organizations with formal or established structure. These included Apollo Group of Hospitals, Fortis Group of

Hospitals, Max Group of Hospitals, Delhi University, SmartAnalyst Inc, Indegene Lifesystems, and Tech Mahindra. They were requested to allow the researcher to collect data. The employees were identified randomly by the researcher across various seniority levels and age groups.

Demographics

The variables related to Employee Demographics were as follows:-

1. Age: Indicative of stage of life cycle, that is, early career (22-27 years), developing career (28-33), consolidating career (34-39), and advanced career (40+).

2. Years of experience: Total number of years of work experience, post education. Education: Graduation, post graduation or doctorate.

3. Cadre: Functional unit based of organization. In the present study, includes associates, managers and senior managers

4. Family type: Includes types like nuclear family, single parent family, joint family, etc.

5. Marital status: The state of being unmarried, married, single parent or others (divorced or separated)

6. Organization type: Refers to the organization being private or public.

7. Sector: Academic, healthcare or corporate services (IT/BPO/KPO).

Average age in present research was 31.5 years. Overall 31% respondents were in 22-27 years age group, 41% were in 28-33 years, 19% were in 34-39 years age group, 9% were in >40 years age group. Average years of experience was 9.1 years. 56% respondents were graduates, and 40% post graduates. 72% were married and 62% had children. Responses were obtained from Apollo hospitals (27), Fortis hospitals (46), Max hospitals (39), Delhi University Colleges (110), SmartAnalyst Inc (24), Indegene Lifesystems (39), and Tech Mahindra (45).

Data Collection

The respondents were either e-mailed or physically given the questionnaires and were allowed comfortable amount of time to complete the responses. Any queries from respondents were timely addressed.

Sampling

Since the population of professionals is infinite, purposeful random sampling was used. Middle level women professionals in different organizations in three different sectors, including academic, healthcare, and corporate were selected for sampling. Questionnaire was sent out to 410 women professionals, out of which 342 responded. 12 responses were discarded after which 330 responses were included in the present study. Formula used to calculate sample size of main research was $N= \{S*Z/ T\}^2$ where S= preliminary standard deviation from pilot study, Z= Confidence level, T= Margin of error. Since S was 14.26, at confidence level of 95%, Z= 1.96, and margin of error of 3%, minimum sample size required was 87. However, since greater sample size is associated with greater precision, questionnaire was sent out to 410 women professionals, out of which 342 responded. 12 responses were discarded after which 330 responses were included in the present study.

Figure 1: Research Model

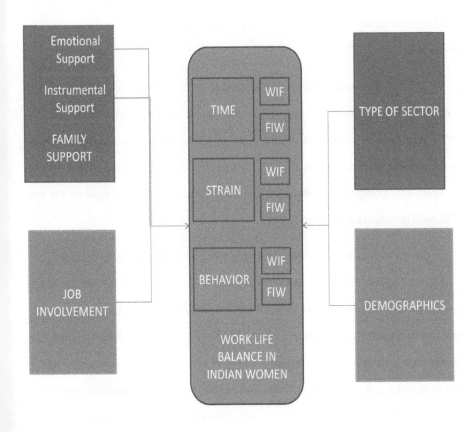

ignou   Work –Life Balance among Women Professionals

Hypotheses

As a dependent variable, WLB has been well researched, but there are limited studies incorporating all the dimensions, and evaluating the effect of independent variables along all directions. This research work attempts to capture variations in perception along all dimensions of WLB due to various independent variables like demographics, sector, family support and job involvement.

Work family conflict (WFC) has been measured in different ways. Initial approach was to conceive WFC in one direction, that is, work interfering with family (Greenhaus & Beutell, 1985). Subsequently, bi directional concept has been researched and adopted, by including both directions: work interfering with family (WIF) and family interfering with work (FIW) (Frone et al., 1992). Thus to completely evaluate WLB, both directions of work–family conflict (WIF and FIW) must be considered (Frone et al., 1992; Greenhaus & Beutell, 1985).

The theorists have also started to study the various forms of work-family conflict (Stephens & Sommer, 1993). In coherence with Greenhaus and Beutell's (1985) definition, three types of work–family conflict have been outlined in theory: (a) time-based conflict, (b) strain-based conflict, and (c) behavior-based conflict. Time-based conflict may happen when time allotted for one role makes it problematic to perform the other role; strain-based conflict reflects that strain observed in a particular role enters into and interferes with performing the other role; and behavior-based conflict happens when certain behaviours for performing a particular role are not in synchronization with what is expectant behaviour in the other role (Greenhaus & Beutell, 1985). Researchers (Gutek, 1991; Carlson, 2000) suggested that each of these three forms of work–family conflict has two directions: (a) conflict due to work interfering with family (WIF) and (b) conflict due to family interfering with work (FIW). When these three forms and two directions are combined six dimensions of work–family conflict result: (1) time-based WIF, (2) time-based FIW, (3) strain-based WIF, (4) strain-based FIW, (5) behavior-based WIF, and (6) behavior-based FIW.

Thus, considering all six dimensions, and two directions, WLB in Indian women was evaluated along and hypothesis generated.

Following were the hypothesis evolved as the pilot was completed and research work progressed

- **Hypothesis 1a: There will be no difference in work life balance in the women professionals, along the time dimension, strain and behavior dimensions**

- **Hypothesis 1b: There will be no difference in work life balance in the women professionals, along the directions WIF and FIW**

- **Hypothesis 1c: There will be no difference in work life balance in the women professionals, along any of the six dimensions of WLB**

Different theorists have observed that based on an individual's period of life, various variables assume varying amounts of significance, and these differing factors influence both work and behaviours in the organization (Giele & Elder, 1998). According to Moen & Yu, 2000, age signifies various situations of life, like, career stage, family stage, maturity, biological aging. Finegold, Mohrman, and Spreitzer (2002) have provided a conceptual reasoning for the importance of impact of age within the relationship of employment. Also results have been obtained by Guest (1998) showing that organizations that meet employees work priorities are more likely to retain their employees and earn their commitment. Hence, as Finegold et al. (2002) concluded that age is just one variable that may influence variations in what employees expect from work and how associated they are to their organization.

.

Roehling, Roehling and Moen's (2001) have elaborated on life-stage model dealing with six unique life-stages, that is, young couple without children or up to 29 years of age with no children living at home; young couples (less than 29 years) with children in the preschool age group that is whose youngest child is five or younger; middle age couples without children or respondents aged 30 - 39 years with no children living at home; mid-age 30–39 year old workers with school aged children or parents whose youngest child is aged between 6 and 17; older non-parents (40-49 years) with no children living at home; and finally respondents (more than 50 years of age) with no children living at home who are preparing for retirement.

In keeping with these findings, this research work tries to consider demographics that may affect work, job and life choices and hence balance. It also attempts to study periods of life based on age depicting unique stages of career and hence, extend the study by looking beyond dependent children and working parents to include a wider definition of work-life balance as it covers all kinds of employees. Thus, four age groupings can be classified to represent various career periods – that is, early career stage from 22-27 years; evolving career stage from 34-39 years; consolidating career stage from 34-39 years; and lastly, advanced career stage from 40+ years onwards.

Following were the hypothesis evolved:

- **H2a: There will be no relationship between years of experience of the respondents and perceived WLB along the three individual dimensions, that is time, strain, and behaviour**
- **H2b: There will be no relationship between years of experience of the respondents and perceived WLB along the two directions that is WIF and FIW**
- **H2c: There will be no relationship between years of experience of the respondents and perceived WLB along any of the six dimensions**
- **H3a: There will be no relationship between age group of the respondents and perceived WLB along the three individual dimensions, that is time, strain, and behaviour**
- **H3b: There will be no relationship between age group of the respondents and perceived WLB along the two directions that is WIF and FIW**
- **H3c: There will be no relationship between age of the respondents and perceived WLB along any of the six dimensions**
- **H4a: There will be no difference due to marital status and WLB along time, strain and behaviour dimensions**
- **H4b: There will be no difference due to marital status and WLB along WIF and FIW directions**
- **H4c: There will be no difference due to marital status and WLB along any of the six dimensions of WLB**
- **H5a: There will be no difference due to presence of children and WLB along time, strain and behaviour dimensions**

ignou   Work –Life Balance among Women Professionals

- **H5b: There will be no difference due to presence of children and WLB along WIF and FIW directions**
- **H5c: There will be no difference due to presence of children and WLB along any of the six dimensions of WLB**

House (1981) indicates that support can increase health and well-being directly, irrespective of stress levels. The hypothesis that support has a direct influence states that all profit from increased amounts of support (House, 1981).

Moreover, the resources-and-demands approach indicates that resources can also help people adjust to demands (Schaufeli and Bakker, 2004). The expectations of work may contain long hours, shift work, frequent travel or job pressure, though private-life expectations are to take care of older relatives and children. Such pressures are not usually negative or conflicting when enough resources are there to meet them (Schaufeli and Bakker, 2004). Schaufeli and Bakker (2004) hence, suggested a negative association between demands and resources in their research, since job resources usually decrease pressures of work.

Studies also suggest role of support from one's life partner. Existing researches indicate both a direct and a cushioning influence of help from one's life partner on work-family conflict (Van Daalen et al., 2006). Other areas of receiving help, such as support from grandparents, friends, neighbours and paid domestic help, are the lesser researched areas.

Other than differentiating between various areas of help, the present studies also differentiates between instrumental and emotional support in the private life and the workplace. Employer work-life programs can be seen as instrumental support in the organization. (Van Daalen et al., 2006, King, 2005). Emotional support, on the other hand, can come from the boss as well as from fellow workers when they show empathy for the person's work-life balance problem. In the private area, emotional help may come from one's life partner, friends, neighbours and relatives. (Van Daalen et al., 2006).

Therefore the following hypothesis is proposed

- **H6a: There will be no relationship between family support or type of family support received by the respondents and perceived WLB along the three dimensions , that is time, strain, and behaviour**
- **H6b: There will be no relationship between family support or type of family support received by the respondents and perceived WLB along the two dimensions , that is time, WIF and FIW**
- **H6c: There will be no relationship between family support or type of family support received by the respondents and perceived WLB along any of the six dimensions**

Job and family involvement measures the extent to which an individual identifies with either family or work roles, and degree of importance of those roles to the person's own image. According to some theories, individuals who are strongly invested in particular roles are much more likely to be aware of and sensitive to the demands and problems of that role (Pleck 1985) and to suffer conflict and role overload if they find they cannot meet their own or others expectations regarding performance in that role (Greenhaus and Beutell 1985).

ignou   Work –Life Balance among Women Professionals

Research indicates high WFC or low balance amongst those individuals who are very involved in their work (Kossek & Ozeki, 1998). On the other hand, several researchers have found a positive relationship between job involvement and work–life imbalance, specifically work–life conflict (Greenhaus & Beutell, 1985). High work involvement and high family involvement have been shown to be positively related to the number of hours spent in work and family activities respectively (Greenhaus & Beutell, 1985).

In coherence with these ideas, earlier studies indicate that concentrating on one's work was positively associated with the other person's judgement about the capability of the manager to progress further as well as real career progression. For instance, 1950s AT&T management progress study evaluated the male managers' low WLB and found it to be positively related to both assessments of the likelihood of promotion to middle management, and management levels attained 8 years later, (Bray, Campbell, & Grant, 1974). In the same fashion, in the AT&T management continuity study conducted between 1977 and 1982 with a more wide sample including women as well as African American and Latino managers, a strong positive association between work involvement factor and evaluations was observed (Howard & Bray, 1988). Ng et al.'s (2005) meta-analytic research with wider samples of employees showed that work focus was positively linked to promotions. In one of the fewer studies that assessed the association between non-work involvement and career advancement for managers, Judiesch and Lyness's (1999) reported that managers taking leaves of absence for family or other reasons received fewer subsequent promotions than did managers who had not taken leaves. Hence as per this perspective, extensive association in either the work or family area has the potential to create conflict across different areas (Greenhaus and Kopelman 1981; Pleck 1985).

ignou   Work –Life Balance among Women Professionals

Kossek and Ozeki (1998) observed from their review of related studies that employees who have greater job involvement tended to experience more WFC. This is contradictory to some studies that report that workers who have high involvement in their jobs are likely to have less concern for their family issues (Kossek & Ozeki, 1988). Thus depending on career stage, high levels of job involvement may increase the likelihood of an individual experiencing work–life imbalance. This is likely to be especially true of individuals at the early and mid-career stage of their careers irrespective of their gender.

Therefore the following hypothesis is proposed:

- **H7a: There will be no relationship between job involvement of the respondents and perceived WLB along the three dimensions , that is time, strain, and behaviour**
- **H7b: There will be no relationship between job involvement of the respondents and perceived WLB along the two dimensions , that is time, WIF and FIW**
- **H7c: There will be no relationship between job involvement of the respondents and perceived WLB along any of the six dimensions.**
- **H8a: There will be no relationship between type of sector of the respondents and perceived WLB along the three dimensions , that is time, strain, and behaviour**
- **H8b: There will be no relationship between type of sector of the respondents and perceived WLB along the two dimensions , that is time, WIF and FIW**
- **H8c: There will be no relationship between type of sector of the respondents and perceived WLB along any of the six dimensions.**

Scales used

Work Life Balance

To measure work-family conflict, WFC scale developed by Carlson, Kacmar and Williams (2000) has been used. The questionnaire is a 18 item scale developed by Carlson et al (2000) with six different subscales that measured the six dimensions of work–family conflict: time-based WIF, time-based FIW, strain-based WIF, strain-based FIW, behavior-based WIF, and behavior-based FIW. (Annexure 1)

Dimensionality was assessed by the authors using a six-factor model where each of the six categories were represented separately. For comparison purposes, three other possible models similar to models used in prior scales were examined- a three-factor model, which represented the three forms of work–family conflict, time, strain, and behaviour; a two-factor model representing the two directions of work–family conflict, and a one-factor model representing a general work–family conflict perspective. (Carlson, 2000) Researchers concluded that the six-factor model is the best fitting model, confirming that questionnaire measure all 3 dimensions (time, strain, behaviour), each in both directions (WIF and FIW). The internal consistency of each of the six dimensions was estimated with coefficient alpha. The reliabilities exceeded the conventional level of acceptance of .70 (Nunnally, 1978): time-based WIF 5 .87; time-based FIW 5 .79; strain based WIF 5 .85; strain-based FIW 5 .87; behavior-based WIF 5 .78; behaviour based FIW 5 .85.(Carlson, 2000)

Other scales exist that measure work–family conflict (i.e., Frone et al., 1992; Gutek et al., 1991), and some have even been subjected to substantial validation efforts (Stephens & Sommer, 1996). However, none of the existing scales provide a way to measure each of the six dimensions of conflict. Stephens and Sommer (1996), whose measure consisted of WIF items, acknowledged that "further study is necessary to adequately measure family to work conflict"

Thus pilot study was used to ensure items were relevant and understood by the respondents, could be validated and showed internal consistency and were non-redundant.

Family support

The questionnaire used was a 44 item scale developed by King, Mattimore et al (1995). It has 2 components: Emotional sustenance and Instrumental assistance.

According to researchers, 44 items (29 emotional sustenance and 15 instrumental assistance) that were selected to comprise the final item set, were those that achieved an item total correlation value equaling or exceeding 0.50 . Additionally, a few items were deleted because their content and wording was judged to be overly redundant with one or more other items. In each case, the deleted item was the one with the lower item-total correlation.

Similar to WLB instrument, pilot study was used to validate the instrument and check internal consistency and inter-item correlation. Overall, 2 items in emotional support subscale were deleted due to low inter item correlation, remaining 42 items- 27 for emotional support and 15 for instrumental support were retained.

Job involvement

The 10 item scale described by Kanungo (1982) and validated by Frone (1995) was used. The original scale developed by Kanungo et al, had two components –job involvement and work involvement. Authors suggested that job involvement section better represents paid work. Within

ignou   Work –Life Balance among Women Professionals

this section, researchers developed three scale- Job involvement semantic differential (8 items), Job involvement (10 items), and Job involvement graphic (1 item) scales. According to Kanungo et al, while semantic differential scale had 'questionable validity' job involvement scale (10item) had highest internal consistency, which was further evaluated and validated by Frone et al, 1995. The scale excludes variables representing emotional state, such as intrinsic motivation. It is also independent of variables like organizational commitment and career commitment, and thus purely measures job involvement. (Frone,1995)

Responses were scored on 5-point Likert scale.

Pilot study also assessed the internal consistency and validity of job involvement instrument, and all 10 items were retained.

Data and Statistical Analysis

Information obtained from demographic profile for respondents was interpreted and analyzed, and for quantitative data, appropriate statistical measures were applied.

For pilot study, cronbach's alpha was calculated for each of the sub-scale, that is, time based work-family (3 items) and family-work (3 items) interface; strain based work- family (3 items) and family-work interface (3 items); behaviour based work-family (3 items) and family-work interface (3 items); emotional support (29 items); instrumental support (15 items);and job involvement (10 items). Inter-item correlation was also calculated for the item within a sub-scale.

Correlation coefficient was calculated between WLB and family support, and between WLB and job involvement. In addition, correlation coefficient was also calculated between WLB and individual components of family support, that is, instrumental support and emotional support. Correlation was also calculated between each of the six dimensions of WLB (time, strain, behaviour along WIF and FIW directions), and the independent variables, that is, job involvement and family support.

.

Pilot Study

The review of literature revealed that standardized tools for work life balance, job involvement and family support, were available. The three questionnaires that were used for final research were also used for pilot- Carlson et al for WLB, King et al for family support, and Kanungo et al for job involvement. Pilot study findings were used for establishing validity, internal consistency and inter item correlation of the three questionnaires, to study the status of WLB and related factors and identify the changes/ additions if any to be done in the main study, was undertaken with 110 women.

WLB instrument validation

Responses were scored on 5-point likert scale. Findings are shown in Table 1. Reliability status with cronbach alpha was- Time based WIF:0.87, Time based FIW: 0.79, Strain based WIF: 0.85, Strain based FIW: 0.87, Behavior based WIF: 0.78, Behavior based FIW: 0.85.

Table 1: Reliability status with cronbach's alpha- WLB scale

S.No	Subscale	Cronbach's alpha
1.	Time based WIF	0.81

2.	Time based FIW	0.83
3.	Strain based WIF	0.86
4.	Strain based FIW	0.85
5.	Behaviour based WIF	0.75
6.	Behaviour based FIW	0.77

According to Gliem et al, inter item correlation and alpha with item deleted, are measures that further help in assessing the reliability and validity of the instrument. Thus inter item correlation (table 2) and alpha without item (table 3) were calculated at the subscale level eg. correlation of item 1 was seen with items 2, and 3, since items 1,2, and 3 were from a common subscale, that is time based WIF.

Table 2: Inter-item correlation at subscale level- WLB

Subscale	Item	Inter-item correlation
Time based WIF	1.	0.6
	2.	0.7
	3.	0.7
Time based FIW	4.	0.7
	5.	0.7
	6.	0.6
Strain based WIF	7.	0.7
	8.	0.8

	9.	0.7
Strain based FIW	10.	0.7
	11.	0.7
	12.	0.7
Behaviour based WIF	13.	0.6
	14.	0.6
	15.	0.6
Behaviour based FIW	16.	0.6
	17.	0.7
	18.	0.5

Table 3: Alpha with item deleted (sub scale level)- WLB

Subscale	Item	Subscale Alpha without item
Time based WIF	1.	0.78
	2.	0.72
	3.	0.7
Time based FIW	4.	0.71
	5.	0.75
	6.	0.84
Strain based WIF	7.	0.83
	8.	0.77
	9.	0.8

ignou   Work –Life Balance among Women Professionals

Strain based FIW	10.	0.81
	11.	0.76
	12.	0.79
Behaviour based WIF	13.	0.64
	14.	0.66
	15.	0.7
Behaviour based FIW	16.	0.65
	17.	0.62
	18.	0.68

Family support instrument validation

As with WLB instrument, pilot was used to validate the instrument for family support.
Responses were scored on 5-point Likert scale. Coefficient alpha for emotional sustenance was
0.87 and for instrumental assistance was 0.89 (table 4). Additionally inter item correlation (table
5) and alpha without item (table 6) was calculated.

Table 4: Reliability status with Cronbach's alpha- family support

S.No	Subscale	Cronbach's alpha
1.	Emotional support	0.87
2.	Instrumental support	0.89

Table 5: Inter item correlation at subscale level –family support

ignou   Work –Life Balance among Women Professionals

Subscale	Item	Inter-item correlation
Emotional support	1.	0.6
	2.	0.5
	3.	0.5
	4.	0.4
	5.	0.4
	6.	0.4
	7.	0.4
	8.	**0.2**
	9.	**0.1**
	10.	0.4
	11.	0.4
	12.	0.4
	13.	0.5
	14.	0.6
	15.	0.5
	16.	0.4
	17.	0.4
	18.	0.4
	19.	0.5
	20.	0.5
	21.	0.5
	22.	0.6

ignou   Work –Life Balance among Women Professionals

	23.	0.5
	24.	0.6
	25.	0.5
	26.	0.5
	27.	0.4
	28.	0.6
	29.	0.5
Instrumental support	30.	0.7
	31.	0.7
	32.	0.6
	33.	0.6
	34.	0.7
	35.	0.5
	36.	0.4
	37.	0.5
	38.	0.6
	39.	0.5
	40.	0.5
	41.	0.5
	42.	0.6
	43.	0.6
	44.	0.5

Table 6: Alpha with item deleted (subscale level)-family support

Subscale	Item	Subscale alpha without item
Emotional support	1.	0.87
	2.	0.86
	3.	0.88
	4.	0.88
	5.	0.87
	6.	0.87
	7.	0.85
	8.	0.88
	9.	0.89
	10.	0.88
	11.	0.88
	12.	0.87
	13.	0.86
	14.	0.88
	15.	0.87
	16.	0.87
	17.	0.87
	18.	0.86
	19.	0.85

ignou   Work –Life Balance among Women Professionals

	20.	0.84
	21.	0.85
	22.	0.85
	23.	0.88
	24.	0.89
	25.	0.88
	26.	0.87
	27.	0.87
	28.	0.87
	29.	0.87
Instrumental support	30.	0.89
	31.	0.90
	32.	0.89
	33.	0.88
	34.	0.90
	35.	0.90
	36.	0.88
	37.	0.88
	38.	0.88
	39.	0.88
	40.	0.87
	41.	0.89

ignou   Work –Life Balance among Women Professionals

	42.	0.90
	43.	0.89
	44.	0.89

2 items, that is item 8- "When I have a tough day at work, family members try to cheer me up* and item 9- "Members of my family are interested in my job* were deleted due to low inter item correlation.

Job involvement instrument validation

As with WLB instrument, pilot was used to validate the instrument for job involvement. Coefficient alpha was 0.8 (table 7). Additionally inter item correlation (table 8) and alpha without item (table 9) was calculated.

Table 7: Reliability status with cronbach's alpha –job involvement

S.No	Scale	Cronbach's alpha
1.	Job involvement	0.8

Table 8: Inter item correlation- job involvement

Scale	Item	Inter-item correlation
Job involvement	1.	0.5
	2.	0.5
	3.	0.5

ignou   Work –Life Balance among Women Professionals

	4.	0.4
	5.	0.4
	6.	0.4
	7.	0.6
	8.	0.6
	9.	0.5
	10.	0.5

Table 9: Alpha with item deleted- job involvement

Scale	Item	Alpha without item
Job involvement	1.	078
	2.	0.78
	3.	0.79
	4.	0.80
	5.	0.79
	6.	0.80
	7.	0.78
	8.	0.76
	9.	0.76
	10.	0.78

Since there was no significant change in apha on any item deletion, inter item correlation was >0.4 for all items, and overall cronbach's alpha was > 0.7 all items were retained and instrument validated. Prior to data analysis, normality distribution was tested using Shapiro-Wilk test for normality which returned non significant (p>0.05), implying distribution was closer to normal distribution, while skewness was <1 and kurtosis < 3. Thus parametric tests could be applied.

Summary: Pilot study validated the three instruments, with 2 items from family support questionnaire being removed, and rest retained. It also helped in evolution of the hypotheses, so the instruments were extended to a larger sample for final tests, and hypotheses tested.

ignou   Work –Life Balance among Women Professionals

CHAPTER -4

ANALYSIS AND INTERPRETATION

ANALYSIS AND INTERPRETATION

Objective 1: To identify the differences between perceived work life balance along each of the individual dimensions of the three dimension, two dimension, and six dimension models of WLB

- **Hypothesis 1a: There will be no difference in work life balance in the women professionals, along the time dimension, strain and behavior dimensions**

  The descriptive statistics of perceived WLB along time, strain and behavior dimensions are tabulated below

Table: 10

Perception of WLB along time, strain and behavior dimensions

No.	Dimension	Item	Mean	N	Std Dev
1.		My work keeps me away from my activities more than I would like	3.87	330	0.58
2.		The time I must devote to my job keeps me from participating equally in household responsibilities and activities.	3.91	330	0.55
3.		I have to miss family activities due to the amount of time I must spend on work responsibilities.	3.84	330	0.58
4.		The time I spend on family responsibilities often interferes with my work responsibilities.	3.04	330	0.52
5.		The time I spend with my family often causes me not to spend time in activities at work that could be helpful for my career.	3.11	330	0.54
6.	Time	I have to miss work activities due to the amount of time I must spend	3.11	330	0.56

ignou   Work –Life Balance among Women Professionals

		on family responsibilities.			
7.		When I get home from work I am often too frazzled (exhausted) to participate in family activities/responsibilities.	3.25	**330**	0.57
8.		I am often so emotionally drained when I get home from work that it prevents me from contributing to my family.	3.25	**330**	0.56
9.		Due to all the pressures at work, sometimes when I come home I am too stressed to do things I enjoy.	3.27	**330**	0.61
10.		Due to stress at home, I am often preoccupied with family matters at work.	2.87	**330**	0.54
11.	Strain	Because I am often too stressed from family responsibilities, I have a hard time concentrating on my work.	2.91	**330**	0.54
12.		Tension and anxiety form my family life often weakens my ability to do my job.	2.83	**330**	0.59
13.		The problem solving behaviors I use in my job are not effective in resolving problems at home.	2.78	**330**	0.65
14.		Behavior that is effective and necessary for me at work would be counterproductive at home.	2.84	**330**	0.59
15.		The behaviors I perform that make me effective at work do not help me to be a better parent and spouse.	2.96	**330**	0.61
16.	Behavior	The behaviors that work for me at home does not seem to be effective at work.	2.79	**330**	0.52
17.		Behavior that is effective and	2.81	**330**	0.50

		necessary for me at home would be counterproductive at work.			
18.		The problem solving behavior that works for me at home does not seem to be useful at work.	2.93	330	0.54

The maximum mean value was 3.91, obtained for "The time I must devote to my job keeps me from participating equally in household responsibilities and activities" (item 2), followed by 3.87 for "My work keeps me away from my activities more than I would like" (item 1). Since Likert was scored as 5 for strongly agree, and 1 for strongly disagree, mean of greater than 3 indicated slight leaning towards agreement for both these items, which were both part of time dimension.

The minimum mean value was 2.78, obtained for "The problem solving behaviors I use in my job are not effective in resolving problems at home" and 2.79 for "The behaviors that work for me at home does not seem to be effective at work." These were both part of behaviour dimension, and values less than 3 indicated slight disagreement with the item.

To assess whether there was an overall difference in the perception of balance/conflict, along the three dimensions, and whether this difference was statistically significant or not, Analysis of Variance (ANOVA) was performed for three dimensions. Since variances were similar, ANOVA could be used.

Table: 11

ANOVA: Single Factor WLB along three dimensions

SUMMARY						
Groups	*Count*	*Sum*	*Average*	*Variance*		

Time	330		6851	20.760	4.468		
Strain	330		6085	18.439	4.885		
Behavior	330		5580	16.909	5.742		
ANOVA							
Source of Variation	Sum of Squares	df	Mean Square	F	P-value	F crit	
Between Groups	1482.042	2	741.0212	73.390	0.000	3.0048	
Within Groups	9966.648	987	10.097				
Total	11448.690	989					

The ANOVA table is divided into between-groups effects and within-group effects. Statistical significance was established by P value, using a cut-off point of 0.05 as criteria for statistical significance.

An F ratio of 73.39 was much higher than F crit of 3.0048. Since P in this case was <0.05, therefore, there was a difference among the perceived WLB for time, strain and behavior dimensions. To locate the group which were having significance differences in mean values, independent samples t-test were done.

Table: 12

t-Test: Two-Sample Assuming Equal Variances- Time and Strain

	Time	*Strain*
Mean	20.760	18.439

Variance	4.4684	4.885
Observations	330	330
Pooled Variance	4.676	
Hypothesized Mean Difference	0	
Df	658	
t Stat	13.787	
P(T<=t) one-tail	0.001	
t Critical one-tail	1.647	
P(T<=t) two-tail	0.001	
t Critical two-tail	1.963	

Thus there was a significant difference between perceived WLB along the time and strain dimensions as P< 0.05.

Table below shows the t –test evaluating the group means along the time and behavior dimensions

Table : 13

t-Test: Two-Sample Assuming Equal Variances- Time and Behavior

	Time	Behaviour
Mean	20.760	16.909
Variance	4.468	5.742
Observations	330	330
Pooled Variance	5.105	
Hypothesized Mean Difference	0	
Df	658	

ignou   Work –Life Balance among Women Professionals

t Stat	21.895	
P(T<=t) one-tail	0.001	
t Critical one-tail	1.817	
P(T<=t) two-tail	0.001	
t Critical two-tail	1.988	

There was a significant difference between perceived WLB along time dimension and behaviour dimension as P < 0.05.

Difference was further evaluated between strain and behaviour dimensions. Table below shows the t –test evaluating the group means along the time and behavior dimensions.

Table: 14

t-Test: Two-Sample Assuming Equal Variances- Strain and Behavior

	Strain	*Behavior*
Mean	18.439	16.909
Variance	4.885	5.742
Observations	330	330
Pooled Variance	5.313	
Hypothesized Mean Difference	0	
Df	658	
t Stat	8.527	
P(T<=t) one-tail	0.002	

t Critical one-tail	1.917	
P(T<=t) two-tail	0.002	
t Critical two-tail	1.993	

There was also a significant difference between perceived WLB along strain and behaviour dimensions. Thus it is clear from statistical analysis that perception of 'balance' or 'conflict' varied along the all three dimensions. These differences were further evaluated along the two dimensions, that is, work- interfering with family (WIF), and family interfering with work (FIW)

- **Hypothesis 1b: There will be no difference in work life balance in the women professionals, along the directions WIF and FIW**

The descriptive statistics of perceived WLB along WIF and FIW are tabulated below.

Table: 15

Perception of WLB along WIF and FIW directions

S.No	Direction		Mean (Subscale level)	N	Std Dev
1	WIF	Time	3.87	990	0.57
		Strain	3.26	990	0.54
		Behaviour	2.88	990	0.58
2	FIW	Time	3.08	990	0.55

ignou   Work –Life Balance among Women Professionals

		Strain	2.88	990	0.50
		Behaviour	2.81	990	0.53

Maximum mean value of 3.87 was obtained for time part of WIF direction (mean of items 1,2,3). Next highest mean value of 3.26, was obtained for strain part of WIF (mean of items 7,8,9). While lowest mean values were obtained in the FIW direction, for behaviour and strain, that is 2.85 (items 16,17,18) and 2.88 (items 10,11,12) respectively.

This implied that there was a difference in perceived WLB between WIF and FIW directions. Mean values > 3 for WIF and <3 for FIW, seemed to suggest slight agreement to items about perception of conflict due to work-interfering with family direction, and slight disagreement to items about family-interfering with work direction.

To ascertain statistical significance of these differences, t test was carried out for WIF and FIW directions.

Table: 16

t-Test: Two-Sample Assuming Equal Variances- WIF and FIW

	WIF	FIW
Mean (Scale level)	30.148	26.490
Variance	8.114	6.449

Observations	330	330
Pooled Variance	7.27	
Hypothesized Mean Difference	0	
Df	658	
t Stat	17.412	
P(T<=t) one-tail	0.000	
t Critical one-tail	1.647	
P(T<=t) two-tail	0.000	
t Critical two-tail	1.963	

Since P in this case was <0.05, therefore, there was a difference among the perceived WLB WIF and FIW directions.

Thus a statistically significant difference in perceived WLB was observed along all three dimensions and both directions.

- **Hypothesis 1c: There will be no difference in work life balance in the women professionals, along any of the six dimensions of WLB**

To further evaluate the source of variation in all six subgroups, the two directions-WIF and FIW were further evaluated within each dimension, that means of time WIF were compared to time FIW, strain WIF to strain FIW, behavior WIF to behavior FIW.

Table below shows the t –test evaluating the group means along the WIF and FIW along time

Table: 17

ignou   Work –Life Balance among Women Professionals

t-Test: Two-Sample – Time-WIF and Time-FIW

	TIME-WIF	TIME-FIW	
Mean	11.607	9.250	
Variance	2.071	1.988	
Observations	330	330	
Pooled Variance	2.029		
Hypothesized Mean Difference	0		
Df	658		
t Stat	20.628		
P(T<=t) one-tail	0.000		
t Critical one-tail	1.647		
P(T<=t) two-tail	0.000		
t Critical two-tail	1.963		

Thus there was a significant different between WIF and FIW along the time dimension, as P <0.05

Similarly Table below shows the t –test evaluating the group means along the WIF and FIW along strain dimension.

Table: 18

ignou   Work –Life Balance among Women Professionals

t-Test: Two-Sample - Strain WIF and Strain FIW

	STRAIN-WIF	STRAIN-FIW
Mean	9.790	8.646
Variance	2.307	2.119
Observations	330	330
Pooled Variance	2.213	
Hypothesized Mean Difference	0	
df	658	
t Stat	9.593	
P(T<=t) one-tail	0.001	
t Critical one-tail	1.647	
P(T<=t) two-tail	0.001	
t Critical two-tail	1.963	

Since P < 0.05, there was a significant difference between WIF and FIW along strain dimension.

Table below shows the t –test evaluating the group means along the WIF and FIW along behavior dimension.

Table: 19

t-Test: Two-Sample –Behavior WIF and Behavior FIW

ignou   Work –Life Balance among Women Professionals

	BEHAVIOR-WIF	BEHAVIOR-FIW
Mean	8.627	8.445
Variance	2.150	1.995
Observations	330	330
Pooled Variance	2.090	
Hypothesized Mean Difference	0	
df	658	
t Stat	1.105	
P(T<=t) one-tail	0.134	
t Critical one-tail	1.648	
P(T<=t) two-tail	0.269	
t Critical two-tail	1.965	

Since P was > 0.05, there was no significant difference between WIF and FIW along the behaviour dimension.

Thus overall there was significant difference in perceived WLB in all three dimensions and two directions.

Within dimensions however, there was a difference between WIF and FIW in time and strain dimension but not in behaviour.

Additionally higher levels of work family conflict were reported along the time-WIF, time-FIW and strain-WIF dimensions, as compared to the other three dimensions in the six dimensional model of the WLB.

Objective 2: To identify the relationship between years of experience and WLB along each of the individual dimensions of the three dimension, two dimension, and six dimension models of WLB

- **H2a: There will be no relationship between years of experience of the respondents and perceived WLB along the three individual dimensions, that is time, strain, and behaviour**

The descriptive statistics of years of experience of the respondents is tabulated below

Table: 20

Proportional distribution of years of experience in each sector

Years of experience	Proportion of respondents (%)

ignou   Work –Life Balance among Women Professionals

	Healthcare	Academic	Corporate services (IT/BPO/KPO)	Total
< 5	35	33	39	36
5-10	42	40	37	40
10-15	14	15	14	14
>15	9	12	10	10

There was a slight variation among different sectors for years of experience. Since due to varying level of educational requirements, years of experience may vary for same age group across sectors, both years of experience and age group were considered separately as independent variables. Average experience of respondents was 9.1 years.

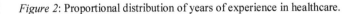

Figure 2: Proportional distribution of years of experience in healthcare.

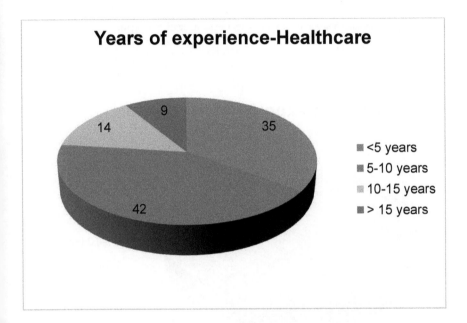

Largest proportion of the respondents in healthcare sector had an experience of 5-10 years, followed by < 5 years group

Mean years of experience were 8.9 years.

Similarly, academic sector respondents had an average of 9 years of experience with largest proportion of respondents being in the 5-10 years group.

Figure 3: Proportional distribution of years of experience in academic sector

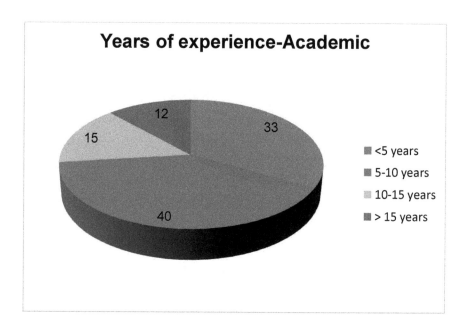

For corporate service (BPO/IT/KPO), largest proportion of respondents were in < 5years age group, followed closely by 5-10 years of age group. Average experience was 9.3 years.

ignou   Work –Life Balance among Women Professionals

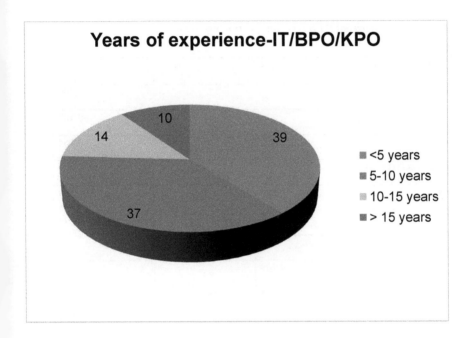

To ascertain any relationship between years of experience and perceived WLB along time, strain and behaviour dimensions, correlation was calculated between years of experience and WLB dimensions. Significance was defined as P< 0.05

Table below shows the results.

Table: 21

Correlation between overall WLB score and years of experience

Correlation Coefficients			
Pearson			-0.209
Spearman			-0.189
Kendall			-0.164
Pearson's coeff (t test)			
Alpha	0.05	Rho	0
Tails	2	Alpha	0.05
		Tails	2
Correlation	-0.209		
Std err	0.098	Correlation	-0.209
T	-2.123	Std err	0.100
p-value	0.036	z	-2.097
Lower	-0.405	p-value	0.035
Upper	-0.013	Lower	-0.390
		Upper	-0.013

ignou   Work –Life Balance among Women Professionals

The results showed a negative correlation between overall score on WLB instrument and years of experience. Thus overall 'imbalance' seemed more in lesser experienced groups.

Further analysis was done along the three individual dimensions, to evaluate the relationship along individual dimensions

Table: 22

Correlation between three dimensions of WLB and years of experience

Correlations					
		Years of experience	Time	Strain	Behavior
Years of experience	Pearson Correlation	-	-0.191	-0.14	0.17
	Sig. (2-tailed)		.003	.008	.75
	N	330	330	330	330
Time	Pearson Correlation	-0.191	-	.112	-.015
	Sig. (2-tailed)	.003		.03	.784

ignou   Work –Life Balance among Women Professionals

		330	330	330	330
Strain	Pearson Correlation	-0.14	.112	-	.082
	Sig. (2-tailed)	.008	.03		.139
	N	330	330	330	330
Behavior	Pearson Correlation	.17	-.015	.082	-
	Sig. (2-tailed)	.75	.784	.139	
	N	330	330	330	330

Years of experience had a weakly negative correlation with time dimension of WLB, which was statistically significant as P< 0.05. Thus greater number of years implied lower score on WLB instrument or lower 'imbalance' or higher conflict along time dimension.

Similar to time dimension, strain dimension also had slight negative correlation with years of experience which was statistically significant. Thus greater the number of years of experience, lesser the imbalance along strain dimension.

There was no significant correlation between behaviour dimension and years of experience

Thus, overall negative correlation between WLB and years of experience was mostly along the time and strain dimensions but not along behvaior dimension.

- **H2b: There will be no relationship between years of experience of the respondents and perceived WLB along the two directions that is WIF and FIW**

To ascertain any relationship between years of experience and perceived WLB along WIF and FIW directions, correlation was calculated between years of experience and two directions. Significance was defined as $P < 0.05$

Table below shows the results.

Table: 23

Correlation of years of experience with WIF and FIW of WLB.

Correlations				
		Years of experience	WIF	FIW
Years of experience	Pearson Correlation	-	-0.151	0.04
	Sig. (2-tailed)		.008	.78
	N	330	330	330

WIF	Pearson Correlation	-0.151	-	.012
	Sig. (2-tailed)	.008		.30
	N	330	330	330
FIW	Pearson Correlation	0.04	.012	-
	Sig. (2-tailed)	.78	.30	
	N	330	330	330

Years of experience had a weakly negative correlation with WIF of WLB, which was statistically significant as P< 0.05. Correlation with FIW was not significant. Thus greater number of years implied lower score on WLB instrument or lower 'imbalance' along WIF

To extrapolate these findings on six dimensional WLB model, a correlation matrix between six dimensions- Time-WIF, Time-FIW, Strain-WIF, Strain-FIW, Behaviour-WIF, Behaviour-FIW and years of experience, was evaluated.

H2c: There will be no relationship between years of experience of the respondents and perceived WLB along any of the six dimensions

Table: 24

Correlation matrix between six dimensions and years of experience

	Years of experience	Time-WIF	Time-FIW	Strain-WIF	Strain-FIW	Behaviour-WIF	Behaviour-FIW
Years of experience	-						
Time-WIF	**-0.286***	-					
Time-FIW	-0.056	0.098	-				
Strain-WIF	**-0.248***	0.031	0.034	-			
Strain-FIW	-0.051	0.013	0.104	0.181	-		
Behaviour-WIF	-0.092	0.068	0.032	0.234	0.177	-	
Behaviour-FIW	0.045	0.119	-0.064	0.080	0.165	0.408	-

*Correlation is significant at 0.05 and 0.01 (2-tailed)

On the six dimensional WLB model, 2 dimensions-time WIF and strain WIF showed statistically significant negative correlation between imbalance and years of age, while other 4 dimensions showed no correlation. Thus lesser experienced respondents perceived most imbalance along time-WIF and strain- WIF dimensions.

Objective 3: To identify the relationship between age group and WLB along each of the individual dimensions of the three dimension, two dimension, and six dimension models of WLB

H3a: There will be no relationship between age group of the respondents and perceived WLB along the three individual dimensions, that is time, strain, and behaviour

The descriptive statistics of years of experience of the respondents is tabulated below

Table: 25

Proportional distribution of age group in each sector

Age group	Proportion of respondents (%)			
	Healthcare	Academic	Corporate services (IT/BPO/KPO)	Total
22-27	28	30	35	31
28-33	44	40	40	41
34-39	19	19	17	19
>40	9	11	8	9

There was a slight variation among different sectors for years of age. Average age of respondents was 31.5 years.

Figure 5: Proportional distribution of age group in healthcare.

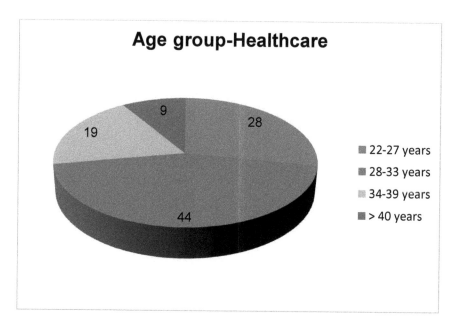

Largest proportion of the respondents in healthcare sector were in the age group 28-33 years followed by 22-27 years group

Mean age was 31.8 years.

Similarly, academic sector respondents had an average of 31.6 years of age with largest proportion of respondents being in the 28-33 years of age group.

ignou   Work –Life Balance among Women Professionals

Figure 6: Proportional distribution of age group in academic sector

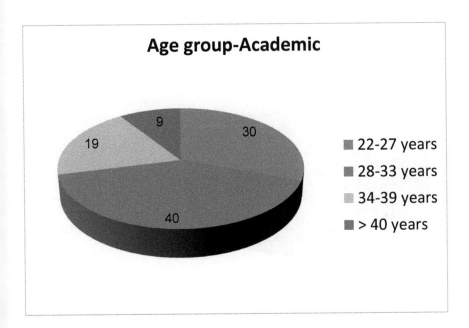

For corporate service (BPO/IT/KPO), similarly, respondents had an average of 30.9 years of age with largest proportion of respondents being in the 28-33 years of age group.

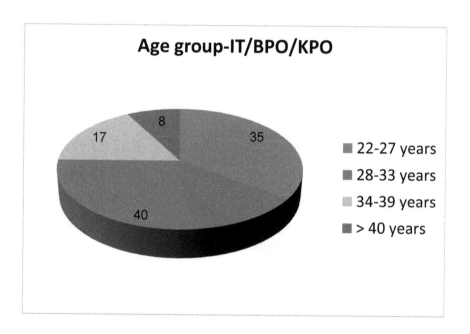

To ascertain any relationship between age group and perceived WLB along time, strain and behaviour dimensions, correlation was calculated between age group and WLB dimensions. Significance was defined as P< 0.05

Table below shows the results.

Table: 26

Correlation between overall WLB score and age

Correlation Coefficients			
Pearson			-0.229
Spearman			-0.205
Kendall			-0.186
Pearson's coeff (t test)			
Alpha	0.05	Rho	0
Tails	2	Alpha	0.05
		Tails	2
Correlation	-0.229		
Std err	0.088	Correlation	-0.229
T	-2.153	Std err	0.090
p-value	0.038	z	-2.157
Lower	-0.427	p-value	0.035
Upper	-0.017	Lower	-0.400
		Upper	-0.018

ignou   Work –Life Balance among Women Professionals

The results showed a negative correlation between overall score on WLB instrument and age group, that was statistically significant. Thus 'imbalance' or conflict seemed more in younger respondents.

Further analysis was done along the three individual dimensions, to evaluate the relationship along individual dimensions

Table below shows the results.

Table: 27

Correlation between three dimensions of WLB and age

Correlations					
		Age	Time	Strain	Behavior
Age	Pearson Correlation	-	**-0.18**	**-0.12**	0.017
	Sig. (2-tailed)		**.003**	**.02**	.32
	N	330	330	330	330
Time	Pearson Correlation	-0.18	-	.112	-.015

	Sig. (2-tailed)	.003		.03	.784
	N	330	330	330	330
Strain	Pearson Correlation	-0.12	.112	-	.082
	Sig. (2-tailed)	.02	.03		.139
	N	330	330	330	330
Behavior	Pearson Correlation	.017	-.015	.082	-
	Sig. (2-tailed)	.32	.784	.139	
	N	330	330	330	330

Age of respondents had a negative correlation with time dimension of WLB, which was statistically significant as $P < 0.05$. Thus greater number of years of age implied lower score on WLB instrument or lower 'imbalance' along time dimension.

Similar to time dimension, strain dimension also had slight negative correlation with years of experience which was statistically significant. Thus greater the age in years, lesser the imbalance along strain dimension. There was no significant correlation between behaviour dimension and age

Thus, overall negative correlation between WLB and age was mostly along the time and strain dimensions.

II3b: There will be no relationship between age group of the respondents and perceived WLB along the two directions that is WIF and FIW

To ascertain any relationship between age and perceived WLB along WIF and FIW directions, correlation was calculated between age and WLB dimensions. Significance was defined as P< 0.05

Table below shows the results.

Table: 28

Correlation of age with WIF and FIW of WLB.

Correlations				
		Age	WIF	FIW
Age in years	Pearson Correlation	-	-0.156	0.014

ignou   Work –Life Balance among Women Professionals

			.008	.18
	Sig. (2-tailed)		.008	.18
	N	330	330	330
WIF	Pearson Correlation	-0.156	-	.012
	Sig. (2-tailed)	.008		.30
	N	330	330	330
FIW	Pearson Correlation	0.014	.012	-
	Sig. (2-tailed)	.18	.30	
	N	330	330	330

Age had negative correlation with WIF of WLB, which was statistically significant as P< 0.05. Thus greater number of years implied lower score on WLB instrument or lower 'imbalance' along WIF. There was no significant correlation between FIW direction and age in years. Thus, there was overall negative correlation between WLB and age group, mostly along the WIF direction.

To extrapolate these findings on six dimensional WLB model, a correlation matrix between six dimensions- Time-WIF, Time-FIW, Strain-WIF, Strain-FIW, Behaviour-WIF, Behaviour-FIW and age in years was evaluated.

H3c: There will be no relationship between age of the respondents and perceived WLB along any of the six dimensions

Table: 29

Correlation matrix between six dimensions and age in years

	Age	Time-WIF	Time-FIW	Strain-WIF	Strain-FIW	Behaviour-WIF	Behaviour-FIW
Age	-						
Time-WIF	**-0.261***	-					
Time-FIW	-0.036	0.098	-				
Strain-WIF	**-0.207***	0.031	0.034	-			
Strain-FIW	-0.071	0.013	0.104	0.181	-		
Behaviour-WIF	-0.082	0.068	0.032	0.234	0.177	1	
Behaviour-FIW	0.051	0.119	-0.064	0.080	0.165	0.408	

*Correlation is significant at 0.05 and 0.01 (2-tailed)

On the six dimensional WLB model, 2 dimensions- time WIF and strain WIF showed moderate negative correlation between imbalance and age group, while other 4 dimensions showed no correlation. Thus both more job experience and age in years showed negative correlation to conflict, with younger and less experienced respondents perceiving greater 'imbalance'

Objective 4: **To identify the differences due to marital status in WLB along each of the individual dimensions of the three dimension, two dimension, and six dimension models of WLB**

H4a: There will be no difference due to marital status and WLB along time, strain and behaviour dimensions

H4b: There will be no difference due to marital status and WLB along WIF and FIW directions

H4c: There will be no difference due to marital status and WLB along any of the six dimensions of WLB

Marital status was divided into married, unmarried, single parent and others (including divorced or separated)

The descriptive statistics are shown below. Most of the respondents were married (72%), while 25 % were in the unmarried group.

Figure 8: Proportional distribution of marital status

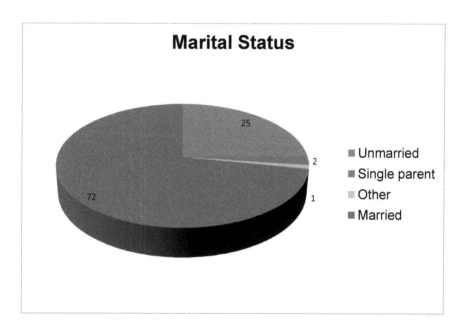

Since marital status is a discontinuous / categorical variable, comparing means of responses was the preferred method of analysis, instead of correlation.

To ascertain any difference due to marital status in perceived WLB along time, strain and behaviour dimensions, t test was performed.

Since number of respondents in single parent and divorced groups were limited, married and unmarried groups were considered for analysis.

ignou   Work –Life Balance among Women Professionals

Table: 30

t-Test: Two-Sample (Married and unmarried)

	Married	Unmarried
Mean	30.33	27.43
Variance	4.11	4.88
Observations	238	83
Pooled Variance	4.48	
Hypothesized Mean Difference	0	
Df	319	
t Stat	14.112	
P(T<=t) one-tail	0.002	
t Critical one-tail	1.64	
P(T<=t) two-tail	0.002	
t Critical two-tail	1.64	

The results showed a statistically significant higher mean value or higher 'imbalance' or conflict in married women as compared to unmarried women..

Since presence of children could have acted as a confounding factor, therefore, to adjust for presence of children, married women without children were considered separately. The table below shoes the findings.

ignou   Work –Life Balance among Women Professionals

Table: 31

t-Test: Two-Sample (Married- without children and unmarried)

	Married (without children)	Unmarried
Mean	29.11	27.43
Variance	4.05	4.88
Observations	91	83
Pooled Variance	4.37	
Hypothesized Mean Difference	0	
df	172	
t Stat	7.062	
P(T<=t) one-tail	0.02	
t Critical one-tail	1.41	
P(T<=t) two-tail	0.02	
t Critical two-tail	1.41	

Thus although adjusting for presence of children, lowered the mean value, the difference was still significant indicating association of marital status with WLB.

To understand the dimensions in which WLB was manifesting in married women (without children), further analysis was performed along each dimension.

Table: 32

ANOVA: Single Factor WLB along three dimensions in married women (without children)

ignou   Work –Life Balance among Women Professionals

SUMMARY							
Groups	*Count*	*Sum*	*Average*	*Variance*			
Time	91	2171	21.49	4.97			
Strain	91	1926	19.06	4.71			
Behavior	91	1785	17.67	4.712			
ANOVA							
Source of Variation	Sum of Squares	df	Mean Square	F	P-value	F crit	
Between Groups	1082.002	2	541.0212	23.78	0.001	3.0048	
Within Groups	6166.75	271	22.752				
Total	7248.752	273					

Overall perceived WLB was in the order time>strain>behaviour. This difference was significant at p<0.05 and p<0.01 Thus marital status increased perception of WLB, will time being the most affected dimension.

Difference was also evaluated between WIF and FIW.

Table: 33

t-Test: Two-Sample WIF and FIW in married women (without children)

	WIF	*FIW*
Mean (Scale level)	31.008	28.110
Variance	7.154	7.739

Observations	91	91
Pooled Variance	7.37	
Hypothesized Mean Difference	0	
df	180	
t Stat	12.412	
P(T<=t) one-tail	0.001	
t Critical one-tail	1.767	
P(T<=t) two-tail	0.001	
t Critical two-tail	1.783	

The WLB perceived was more in WIF dimension than in FIW dimension, and this difference was significant at p<0.01

To further evaluate the source of variation in all six subgroups, the two directions-WIF and FIW were further evaluated within each dimension, such that means of time WIF were compared to time FIW, strain WIF to strain FIW, behavior WIF to behavior FIW.

Table below shows the t –test evaluating the group means along the WIF and FIW along time

Table: 34

t-Test: Two-Sample – Time-WIF and Time-FIW in married women (without children)

	TIME-WIF	TIME-FIW	
Mean	11.886	9.975	

ignou   Work –Life Balance among Women Professionals

Variance	2.121	1.798	
Observations	91	91	
Pooled Variance	1.978		
Hypothesized Mean Difference	0		
Df	180		
t Stat	10.438		
P(T<=t) one-tail	0.01		
t Critical one-tail	1.817		
P(T<=t) two-tail	0.01		
t Critical two-tail	1.883		

Thus there was a significant different between WIF and FIW along the time dimension, as P <0.05

Similarly Table below shows the t –test evaluating the group means along the WIF and FIW along strain dimension.

Table: 35

t-Test: Two-Sample - Strain WIF and Strain FIW in married women (without children)

	STRAIN-WIF	STRAIN-FIW
Mean	10.210	9.346

ignou   Work –Life Balance among Women Professionals

		2.217	2.229
Variance		2.217	2.229
Observations		91	91
Pooled Variance		2.223	
Hypothesized Mean Difference		0	
df		180	
t Stat		7.213	
P(T<=t) one-tail		0.01	
t Critical one-tail		1.847	
P(T<=t) two-tail		0.001	
t Critical two-tail		1.983	

Since P < 0.05, there was a significant difference between WIF and FIW along strain dimension.

Table below shows the t –test evaluating the group means along the WIF and FIW along behavior dimension.

Table: 36

t-Test: Two-Sample –Behavior WIF and Behavior FIW

	BEHAVIOR-WIF	BEHAVIOR-FIW
Mean	8.987	8.775
Variance	2.250	1.985
Observations	91	91

Pooled Variance	2.095	
Hypothesized Mean Difference	0	
Df	180	
t Stat	1.115	
P(T<=t) one-tail	0.134	
t Critical one-tail	1.668	
P(T<=t) two-tail	0.269	
t Critical two-tail	1.995	

Since P was > 0.05, there was no significant difference between WIF and FIW along the behaviour dimension.

Thus overall marital status resulted in significant difference in perceived WLB which was played out mainly in time, and WIF dimensions.

Additionally, in the six dimensional model, higher levels of work family conflict due to being married, were reported along the time-WIF, and strain-WIF dimensions, as compared to the other four dimensions.

Objective 5: To identify the differences in WLB along each of the individual dimensions of the three dimension, two dimension, and six dimension models of WLB, due presence of children

ignou   Work –Life Balance among Women Professionals

- **H5a: There will be no difference due to presence of children and WLB along time, strain and behaviour dimensions**
- **H5b: There will be no difference due to presence of children and WLB along WIF and FIW directions**
- **H5c: There will be no difference due to presence of children and WLB along any of the six dimensions of WLB**

Groups considered for initial analysis and comparison of means were-- 'married with children', and 'married without children.' Married (72%) respondents were divided into two groups- with children group (62%) and without children group (38%). Single parents were not added to this pool, or considered separately due to small sample size (2% or 7 respondents), and to avoid confounding.

Age group of children was not considered for analysis.

Figure 9: Proportional distribution of presence of children

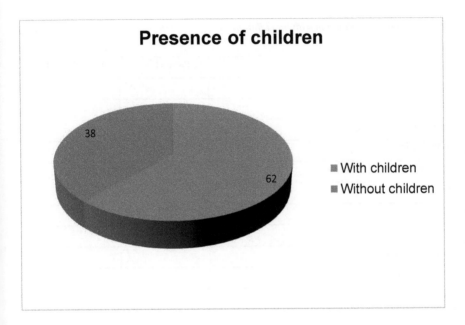

Since presence or absence of children is a discontinuous / categorical variable, comparing means of responses was the preferred method of analysis, instead of correlation.

To ascertain any difference due to presence of children in perceived WLB along time, strain and behaviour dimensions, t test was performed.

Table: 37

t-Test: Two-Sample (With and without children)

	Without children	With children
Mean	30.33	31.93
Variance	4.11	4.38
Observations	101	147
Pooled Variance	4.24	
Hypothesized Mean Difference	0	
Df	248	
t Stat	5.012	
P(T<=t) one-tail	0.02	
t Critical one-tail	1.77	
P(T<=t) two-tail	0.02	
t Critical two-tail	1.70	

The results showed a statistically significant higher mean value or higher 'imbalance' or conflict in respondents with children as compared to those without children.

To understand the dimensions in which WLB was manifesting in respondent with children, further analysis was performed along each dimension.

Table: 38

ANOVA: Single Factor WLB along three dimensions in respondents (with children)

SUMMARY						
Groups	*Count*	*Sum*	*Average*	*Variance*		

Time	147	3321	22.59	4.44		
Strain	147	2955	20.10	4.23		
Behavior	147	2789	18.97	4.212		
ANOVA						
Source of Variation	Sum of Squares	df	Mean Square	F	P-value	F crit
Between Groups	1072.002	2	536.001	20.73	0.011	3.0468
Within Groups	11346.26	439	25.85			
Total	12418.262	441				

Overall perceived conflict along the dimensions time>strain>behaviour. This difference was significant at p<0.05 Thus presence of children increased perception of WLB, will time being the most affected dimension.

Difference was also evaluated between WIF and FIW.

Table: 39

t-Test: Two-Sample WIF and FIW in respondents (with children)

	WIF	*FIW*
Mean (Scale level)	32.108	31.610
Variance	6.78	6.974
Observations	147	147

ignou   Work –Life Balance among Women Professionals

Pooled Variance	6.88	
Hypothesized Mean Difference	0	
df	292	
t Stat	1.412	
P(T<=t) one-tail	0.113	
t Critical one-tail	1.767	
P(T<=t) two-tail	0.120	
t Critical two-tail	1.783	

There was no significant difference in WLB perceived along WIF and FIW, in parent responders. Thus family seemed to interfere as much in work (FIW), as work was perceived to interfere with family domain (WIF).

To further evaluate any variation in all six subgroups, the two directions-WIF and FIW were further evaluated within each dimension, such that means of time WIF were compared to time FIW, strain WIF to strain FIW, behavior WIF to behavior FIW.

Table below shows the t –test evaluating the group means along the WIF and FIW along time

Table: 40

t-Test: Two-Sample – Time-WIF and Time-FIW in respondents (with children)

	TIME-WIF	TIME-FIW	
Mean	12.086	11.978	

ignou   Work –Life Balance among Women Professionals

Variance	2.151	1.998	
Observations	147	147	
Pooled Variance	2.024		
Hypothesized Mean Difference	0		
Df	292		
t Stat	1.498		
P(T<=t) one-tail	0.21		
t Critical one-tail	1.717		
P(T<=t) two-tail	0.22		
t Critical two-tail	1.643		

Table: 41

t-Test: Two-Sample - Strain WIF and Strain FIW in respondents (with children)

	STRAIN-WIF	STRAIN-FIW
Mean	11.010	10.346
Variance	2.117	2.369
Observations	147	147
Pooled Variance	2.263	
Hypothesized Mean Difference	0	

ignou   Work –Life Balance among Women Professionals

Df	292	
t Stat	1.213	
P(T<=t) one-tail	0.16	
t Critical one-tail	1.891	
P(T<=t) two-tail	0.18	
t Critical two-tail	1.783	

Table: 42

t-Test: Two-Sample –Behavior WIF and Behavior FIW in respondents (with children)

	BEHAVIOR-WIF	BEHAVIOR-FIW
Mean	9.869	9.785
Variance	2.120	2.185
Observations	147	147
Pooled Variance	2.165	
Hypothesized Mean Difference	0	
Df	292	
t Stat	1.45	
P(T<=t) one-tail	0.134	
t Critical one-tail	1.78	
P(T<=t) two-tail	0.269	

ignou   Work –Life Balance among Women Professionals

t Critical two-tail	1.95	

Analysis along six dimensions showed no difference between WIF and FIW along time, strain and behaviour dimensions. Since it could also imply conflict was perceived along both WIF and FIW dimensions, a dimension wise comparison was done with WLB experienced by 'no children' group.

Table: 43

t-Test: Two-Sample Assuming Equal Variances (with and without children) for time dimension

	With children	Without children
Mean	20.16	18.67
Variance	4.14	4.07
Observations	147	91
Pooled Variance	4.10	
Hypothesized Mean Difference	0	
Df	236	
t Stat	12.112	
P(T<=t) one-tail	0.009	
t Critical one-tail	1.55	
P(T<=t) two-tail	0.009	
t Critical two-tail	1.55	

ignou   Work –Life Balance among Women Professionals

Thus respondents with children showed significantly lower overall 'balance' than those without children, along time dimension.

Table: 44

t-Test: Two-Sample Assuming Equal Variances (with and without children) for strain dimension

	With children	Without children
Mean	20.02	18.58
Variance	4.04	4.08
Observations	147	91
Pooled Variance	4.06	
Hypothesized Mean Difference	0	
Df	236	
t Stat	12.2	
P(T<=t) one-tail	0.029	
t Critical one-tail	1.41	
P(T<=t) two-tail	0.029	
t Critical two-tail	1.41	

Table: 45 -t-Test: Two-Sample Assuming Equal Variances (with and without children) for behaviour dimension

ignou   Work –Life Balance among Women Professionals

	With children	Without children
Mean	19.02	19.16
Variance	4.04	4.08
Observations	147	91
Pooled Variance	4.06	
Hypothesized Mean Difference	0	
Df	236	
t Stat	1.32	
P(T<=t) one-tail	0.23	
t Critical one-tail	1.41	
P(T<=t) two-tail	0.23	
t Critical two-tail	1.41	

Thus respondents with children also showed statistically significantly lower overall 'balance' than those without children, along strain dimension as well. There was no difference in perceived WLB along behaviour dimension.

Differences along WIF and FIW were also evaluated.

Table: 46

t-Test: Two-Sample Assuming Equal Variances (with and without children) WIF

	With children	Without children
Mean	20.07	19.71
Variance	4.23	4.17
Observations	147	91
Pooled Variance	4.19	
Hypothesized Mean Difference	0	

ignou   Work –Life Balance among Women Professionals

Df	236	
t Stat	13.2	
P(T<=t) one-tail	0.03	
t Critical one-tail	1.3	
P(T<=t) two-tail	0.03	
t Critical two-tail	1.3	

Table: 47

t-Test: Two-Sample Assuming Equal Variances (with and without children) FIW

	With children	Without children
Mean	19.47	19.32
Variance	4.44	4.32
Observations	147	91
Pooled Variance	4.38	
Hypothesized Mean Difference	0	
Df	236	
t Stat	10.2	
P(T<=t) one-tail	0.03	
t Critical one-tail	1.45	
P(T<=t) two-tail	0.03	
t Critical two-tail	1.55	

ignou   Work –Life Balance among Women Professionals

Thus perceived WLB was greater in 'with children' along time, strain, WIF and FIW dimensions, as compared to 'without children' respondents.

Objective 6: To identify the relationship between family support or type of family support received by the respondents and WLB along each of the individual dimensions of the three dimension, two dimension, and six dimension models of WLB

The descriptive statistics of perceived family support along emotional and instrumental components are tabulated below

Table: 48

Family support received- emotional and instrumental components

NO	TYPE	ITEMS	Mean	N	Std. Dev
1.		When I succeed at work, members of my family show that they are proud of me*	2.97	330	0.65
2.		My family members do not seem very interested in hearing about my work day	3.01	330	0.59
3.		When something at work is bothering me, members of my family show that they understand how I'm feeling*	3.10	330	0.61
4.		When I talk with them about my work, my family members don't really listen	3.55	330	0.52

5.	Emotional Support	Someone in my family asks me regularly about my work day*	**3.77**	330	0.50
6.		As long as I'm making money, it doesn't really matter to members of my family what job I have	**3.67**	330	0.54
7.		I feel better after discussing job-related problems with a family member*	3.03	330	0.65
8.		I have difficulty discussing work-related activities with members of my family	3.17	330	0.59
9.		When I'm frustrated by my work, someone in my family tries to understand*	3.23	330	0.61
10.		Members of my family always seem to make time for me if I need to discuss my work*	3.22	330	0.54
11.		I wish members of my family would care more about what I do at work	2.85	330	0.54
12.		Members of my family often provide a different way of looking at my work-related problems*	2.88	330	0.59
13.	Emotional Support	Members of my family don't want to listen to my work-related problems	3.08	330	0.65
14.		Members of my family seem bored when I talk about my job	2.74	330	0.59
15.		Members of my family have little respect for my job	3.1	330	0.61
16.		Members of my family are happy for me when I am successful at work*	2.95	330	0.52
17.		Someone in my family helps me feel better when I'm upset about my job*	3.11	330	0.50

18.		I usually find it useful to discuss my work problems with family members*	3.12	330	0.54
19.		Members of my family want me to enjoy my job*	3.1	330	0.50
20.		Members of my family enjoy hearing about my achievements at work*	3.06	330	0.54
21.		My family members have a positive attitude toward my work*	3.12	330	0.65
22.		When I have a problem at work, my family members seem to blame me	3.15	330	0.59
23.		When I have a problem at work, members of my family express concern*	3.09	330	0.61
24.		I look to family members for reassurance about my job when I need it*	3.02	330	0.54
25.		I feel comfortable asking members of my family for advice about a problem situation at work*	2.94	330	0.54
26.		My family members are sympathetic when I'm upset about my work*	2.76	330	0.50
27.		If I have a problem at work, I usually share it with my family members*	2.79	330	0.50
28.		My family members burden me with things that they should be able to handle on their own	2.69	330	0.54
29.		Members of my family cooperate with me to get things done around the house*	2.88	330	0.65
30.		If I had to go out of town for my job, my family would have a hard time managing household responsibilities	3.03	330	0.59

ignou   Work –Life Balance among Women Professionals

31.		It seems as if my family members are always demanding me to do something for them	3.53	330	0.61
32.	Instrumental Support	My family members do their fair share of household chores*	2.94	330	0.52
33.		Members of my family are willing to straighten up the house when it needs it*	2.77	330	0.50
34.		My family leaves too much of the daily details of running the house to me	3.20	330	0.54
35.		Someone in my family helps me out by running errands when necessary*	3.13	330	0.65
36.		If my job gets very demanding, someone in my family will take on extra household responsibilities*	2.94	330	0.65
37.		My family members give me too much responsibility for household repairs and maintenance	3.21	330	0.59
38.		I can depend on members of my family to help me out when I'm running late for work*	2.78	330	0.61
39.		Members of my family help me with routine household tasks*	2.90	330	0.60
40.		If I have to work late, I can count on someone in my family to take care of everything at home*	2.79	330	0.51
41.		Too much of my time at home is spent picking up after my family members	2.77	330	0.49
42.		When I'm having a difficult week at my job, my family members try to do more of the work around the house*	2.81	330	0.44

Emotional support component had 27 items. The maximum mean value was 3.77, obtained for "Someone in my family asks me regularly about my work day" (item 5), followed by 3.67 for "As long as I'm making money, it doesn't really matter to members of my family what job I have" (item 6). Since Likert was scored as 5 for strongly agree, and 1 for strongly disagree, for items with asterisk, these responses indicated general agreement for item 5 and general disagreement for item 6.

Minimum value of 2.69 was achieved for instrumental support item "My family members burden me with things that they should be able to handle on their own". Since items without asterisk were reverse coded, this indicated agreement for item 28.

- **H6a: There will be no relationship between family support or type of family support received by the respondents and perceived WLB along the three dimensions , that is time, strain, and behaviour**
- **H6b: There will be no relationship between family support or type of family support received by the respondents and perceived WLB along the two dimensions , that is time, WIF and FIW**

To assess if there was any difference between two subscales, independent samples T test was done

Table: 49

t-Test: Two-Sample Assuming Equal Variances- Received emotional and instrumental support

	Emotional Support	Instrumental Support
Mean	3.21	2.91
Variance	0.55	0.48
Observations	330	330
Pooled Variance	0.51	
Hypothesized Mean Difference	0	
Df	658	
t Stat	10.7873	
P(T<=t) one-tail	0.03	
t Critical one-tail	1.6	
P(T<=t) two-tail	0.03	
t Critical two-tail	1.9	

Thus p value was < 0.05, indicating significant difference between the type of support received, overall perceived emotional support was greater than perceived instrumental support.

ignou   Work –Life Balance among Women Professionals

To ascertain any relationship between family support and perceived WLB along time, strain and behaviour dimensions, correlation was calculated between presence of children and WLB dimensions. Significance was defined as $P < 0.05$

Table: 50

Correlation between three dimensions of WLB and family support

	Family support	Instrumental support	Emotional support	Time	Strain	Behaviour
Family support	-					
Instrumental support	0.15	-				
Emotional support	0.21	0.15	-			
Time	**-0.21***	**-0.30****	-0.10	-		
Strain	**-0.15***	**-0.25****	-0.10	0.02	-	
Behaviour	0.04	0.01	0.02	0.02	0.03	-

* Correlation is significant at 0.05 (2-tailed)

** Correlation is significant at 0.01 (2-tailed)

ignou   Work –Life Balance among Women Professionals

Table: 51

Correlation between two dimensions of WLB and family support

	Family support	Instrumental support	Emotional support	WIF	FIW
Family support	-				
Instrumental support	0.15	-			
Emotional support	0.21	0.15	-		
WIF	-0.11*	-0.23**	0.02	-	
FIW	-0.22*	-0.29**	-0.19*	0.04	-

* Correlation is significant at 0.05 (2-tailed)

** Correlation is significant at 0.01 (2-tailed)

Thus overall family support had negative correlation with 'imbalance' along the time and strain dimensions. In addition, moderate negative correlation was seen in FIW direction, implying less interference of family in work, when they were supportive.

Correlation was stronger for instrumental component than emotional component, and this difference was significant. Instrumental component showed negative correlation in time, strain, WIF and FIW, that is, four out of six dimensions.

Emotional support showed some correlation only in one dimension, that is, FIW indicating somewhat decreased interference by family in work.

To extrapolate these findings on six dimensional WLB model, a correlation matrix between six dimensions- Time-WIF, Time-FIW, Strain-WIF, Strain-FIW, Behaviour-WIF, Behaviour-FIW and age in years was evaluated.

- **H6c: There will be no relationship between family support or type of family support received by the respondents and perceived WLB along any of the six dimensions**

Table: 52

Correlation matrix between six dimensions and family support

Table below shows the results.

	Instrumental support	Emotional support	Time-WIF	Time-FIW	Strain-WIF	Strain-FIW	Behaviour- WIF	Behaviour-FIW
Instrumental support	-							

ignou   Work –Life Balance among Women Professionals

Emotional support	0.16	-						
Time-WIF	-0.33**	-0.11	-					
Time-FIW	-0.20*	-0.07	0.01	-				
Strain-WIF	-0.28**	-0.11	0.02	0.04	-			
Strain-FIW	-0.17*	-0.06	0.02	0.05	0.03	-		
Behaviour-WIF	0.01	0.02	0.01	0.04	0.03	0.03	-	
Behaviour-FIW	0.04	0.02	0.03	0.03	0.02	0.03	0.05	-

* Correlation is significant at 0.05 (2-tailed)

** Correlation is significant at 0.01 (2-tailed)

The results showed a moderately negative correlation between 'imbalance' or conflict and instrumental support particularly along Time-WIF, Time-FIW and Strain –WIF and Strain- FIW, that is more the instrumental support, less was the conflict experienced by the respondents.

However, emotional support did not show significant correlation with WLB.

Objective 7: To identify the relationship between job involvement of the respondents and WLB along each of the individual dimensions of the three dimension, two dimension, and six dimension models of WLB

- **H7a:** There will be no relationship between job involvement of the respondents and perceived WLB along the three dimensions , that is time, strain, and behaviour
- **H7b:** There will be no relationship between job involvement of the respondents and perceived WLB along the two dimensions , that is time, WIF and FIW
- **H7c:** There will be no relationship between job involvement of the respondents and perceived WLB along any of the six dimensions.

The descriptive statistics of perceived job involvement are tabulated below

Table: 53

Job involvement questionnaire

NO	TYPE	ITEMS	Mean	N	Std. Dev
1.		The most important things that happen to me involve my present job.	3.38	330	0.49
2.		Most of my interests are centered on my job.	2.94	330	0.59
3.	Job involvement	To me, my job is a very large part of who I am.	2.96	330	0.63

4.		I am very much personally involved with my job.	3.77	330	0.62
5.		My job is a very important part of my life.	3.68	330	0.55
6.		I live, eat and breathe my job.	2.91	330	0.54
7.		I have very strong ties with my present job which would be very difficult to break	3.18	330	0.63
8.		Usually I feel detached from my job*	3.22	330	0.59
9.		Most of my personal life goals are job-oriented	3.28	330	0.67
10.		I like to be really involved in my job most of the time	2.95	330	0.64

Job involvement questionnaire had 10 items. The maximum mean value of 3.77 was achieved for item 4-"I am very much personally involved with my job" indicating general agreement. Next highest mean value of 3.68 was achieved for "My job is a very important part of my life" indicating general agreement.

The minimum mean value of 2.81 was achieved for item 6, "I live eat and breath my job" indicating general disagreement.

To ascertain any relationship between job involvement (JI) and perceived WLB along time, strain and behaviour dimensions, correlation was calculated between JI and WLB dimensions. Significance was defined as $P< 0.05$

Table: 54

Correlation between three dimensions of WLB and job involvement

	Job involvement	Time	Strain	Behaviour
Job involvement	-			
Time	**0.24***	-		
Strain	**0.20***	0.02	-	
Behaviour	0.08	0.02	0.03	-

* Correlation is significant at 0.05 (2-tailed)

Table: 55

Correlation between two directions of WLB and job involvement

	Job involvement	WIF	FIW
Job involvement	-		

WIF	0.10	-
FIW	0.11	0.04	-

Thus overall job involvement had positive correlation with 'imbalance' along the time and strain dimensions. However, there was no significant correlation with either WIF or FIW directions. Further analysis was done along the six dimensional model of WLB.

Table: 56

Correlation matrix between six dimensions and job involvement

	Job involvem ent	Time-WIF	Time-FIW	Strain-WIF	Strain-FIW	Behaviou r- WIF	Behaviou r-FIW
Job involveme nt	-						
Time-WIF	0.21*	-					
Time-FIW	0.27*	0.01	-				
Strain-WIF	0.20*	0.02	0.04	-			

	0.19*	0.02	0.05	0.03	-		
Strain-FIW							
Behaviour-WIF	0.08	0.01	0.04	0.03	0.03	-	
Behaviour-FIW	0.09	0.03	0.03	0.02	0.03	0.05	-

* Correlation is significant at 0.05 (2-tailed)

The results showed a moderately positive correlation between 'imbalance' or conflict and job involvement particularly along Time-WIF, Time-FIW and Strain –WIF and Strain- FIW, directions. Thus greater job involvement was associated with greater 'imbalance'

Objective 8: To identify the relationship between type of sector of the respondents and WLB along each of the individual dimensions of the three dimension, two dimension, and six dimension models of WLB

- **H8a: There will be no relationship between type of sector of the respondents and perceived WLB along the three dimensions , that is time, strain, and behaviour**

- **H8b: There will be no relationship between type of sector of the respondents and perceived WLB along the two dimensions , that is time, WIF and FIW**

- **H8c: There will be no relationship between type of sector of the respondents and perceived WLB along any of the six dimensions.**

Respondents were pooled from academic, healthcare and corporate services (BPO/KPO/IT).

The descriptive statistics are shown below.

Table: 57

Descriptive statistics for healthcare, corporate services and academic sectors

Demographics	Parameter	Sector			
		Healthcare	Academic	Corporate services (IT/BPO/KPO)	Total
Number		112	110	108	330
Education (%)	Graduates	54	51	60	56
	Post graduates	44	47	38	40
	Doctoral/ Additional	1.7	2	1.3	14

Figure 10: Proportional distribution of level of education-healthcare

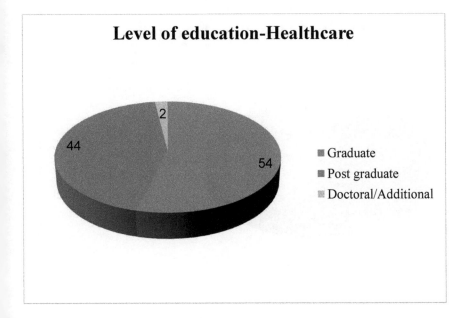

Level of education-Healthcare

2

44

54

■ Graduate
■ Post graduate
■ Doctoral/Additional

Figure 11: Proportional distribution of level of education-academic

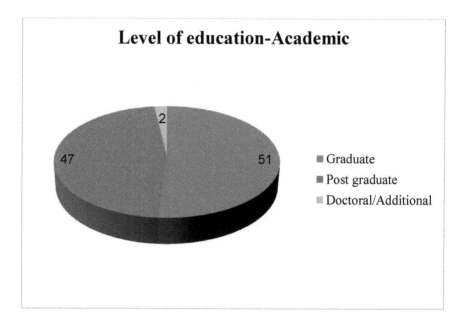

Level of education-Academic

2

47   51   ▪ Graduate
            ▪ Post graduate
            ▪ Doctoral/Additional

Figure 12: Proportional distribution of level of education-corporate services

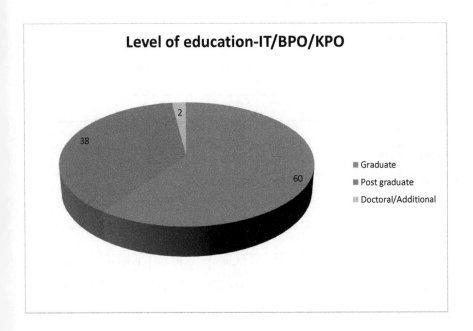

While respondents with qualifications greater than post graduation were similar in three sectors, graduates formed the largest proportion in all three sectors, and were most prominent subgroup in IT/BPO/KPO sector.

Since sector is a discontinuous / categorical variable, comparing means of responses was the preferred method of analysis, instead of correlation.

To test for overall difference in WLB score between three groups, ANOVA was applied.

ignou   Work –Life Balance among Women Professionals

Table: 58

ANOVA for WLB across all three groups

ANOVA: Single Factor

SUMMARY						
Groups	*Count*	*Sum*	*Average*	*Variance*		
Corporate services	108	3322	30.760	4.68		
Academic	110	2908	26.439	4.85		
Healthcare	112	3236	28.909	5.42		
ANOVA						
Source of Variation	Sum of Squares	df	Mean Square	F	P-value	F crit
Between Groups	1106.04	2	553.02	17.61	0.01	3.018
Within Groups	10266.64	327	31.39			
Total	8048.6909	329				

Since P value was < 0.05, there was a difference in overall WLB across groups based on marital status. Mean score on WLB instrument showed corporate services> healthcare> academic, for perceived imbalance.

Subscale level/ dimension wise analysis was done to understand variations within each sector along WLB dimensions.

Sector wise variations along three dimensions

Table: 59

ANOVA: Single Factor WLB along three dimensions in corporate services

SUMMARY							
Groups	*Count*	*Sum*	*Average*	*Variance*			
Time	108	2469	22.86	4.44			
Strain	108	2284	21.15	4.23			
Behavior	108	2084	19.30	4.12			
ANOVA							
Source of Variation	Sum of Squares	df	Mean Square	F	P-value	F crit	
Between Groups	672.002	2	336.001	8.117	0.000	3.048	
Within Groups	4346.26	105	41.39				
Total	5018.262	107					

ignou   Work –Life Balance among Women Professionals

Overall perceived conflict along the dimensions time>strain>behaviour. This difference was significant at p<0.05 Thus within corporate service, WLB was perceived differently across different dimension, with time being the most affected dimension.

Table: 60

ANOVA: Single Factor WLB along three dimensions in academic sector

SUMMARY						
Groups	*Count*	*Sum*	*Average*	*Variance*		
Time	110	2382	21.66	4.24		
Strain	110	2161	19.65	4.23		
Behavior	110	1894	17.22	4.01		
ANOVA						
Source of Variation	Sum of Squares	df	Mean Square	F	P-value	F crit
Between Groups	602	2	301	7.37	0.001	3.048
Within Groups	4366	107	40.80			
Total	4968	109				

Table: 61

ANOVA: Single Factor WLB along three dimensions in healthcare sector

SUMMARY						
Groups	*Count*	*Sum*	*Average*	*Variance*		

ignou   Work –Life Balance among Women Professionals

Time	112		2484	22.18	4.33		
Strain	112		2264	20.22	4.38		
Behavior	112		2049	18.30	4.12		
ANOVA							
Source of Variation	Sum of Squares	df	Mean Square	F	P-value	F crit	
Between Groups	632	2	316	8.600	0.001	3.048	
Within Groups	4005	109	36.743				
Total	4637	111					

Thus time dimension had the highest mean in all sectors, and difference between perception of WLB, in terms of dimensions, was significant in all three sectors. Overall time> strain >behaviour.

Difference was also evaluated between WIF and FIW.

Table:62

t-Test: Two-Sample WIF and FIW in corporate services

	WIF	FIW
Mean (Scale level)	32.33	31.010
Variance	6.08	6.00
Observations	108	108
Pooled Variance	6.88	
Hypothesized Mean Difference	0	

ignou   Work –Life Balance among Women Professionals

df	214	
t Stat	5.612	
P(T<=t) one-tail	0.011	
t Critical one-tail	1.671	
P(T<=t) two-tail	0.012	
t Critical two-tail	1.683	

There was a significant difference in WLB perceived along WIF and FIW, in respondents from corporate services including BPO, KPO, and IT

Table: 63

t-Test: Two-Sample WIF and FIW in academic sector

	WIF	FIW
Mean (Scale level)	30.66	29.81
Variance	5.78	5.65
Observations	110	110
Pooled Variance	5.71	
Hypothesized Mean Difference	0	
df	218	
t Stat	1.612	
P(T<=t) one-tail	0.311	

t Critical one-tail	1.871	
P(T<=t) two-tail	0.32	
t Critical two-tail	1.883	

There was no significant difference in WLB perceived along WIF and FIW, in respondents from academic sector.

Table: 64

t-Test: Two-Sample WIF and FIW in healthcare sector

	WIF	FIW
Mean (Scale level)	31.81	29.91
Variance	6.08	6.05
Observations	112	112
Pooled Variance	6.06	
Hypothesized Mean Difference	0	
df	222	
t Stat	4.354	
P(T<=t) one-tail	0.026	
t Critical one-tail	1.771	
P(T<=t) two-tail	0.022	
t Critical two-tail	1.763	

There was a significant difference in WLB perceived along WIF and FIW, in respondents from healthcare sector.

ignou   Work –Life Balance among Women Professionals

Thus, in the two dimension model, WIF >FIW for corporate services and healthcare, but not for academic sector. Thus WLB was differentially perceived in two out of three sectors, as far as two dimension model is concerned.

To further evaluate any variation in all six subgroups, the two directions-WIF and FIW were further evaluated within each dimension, such that means of time WIF were compared to time FIW, strain WIF to strain FIW, behavior WIF to behavior FIW.

Table below shows the t –test evaluating the group means along the WIF and FIW along time

Table: 65

t-Test: Two-Sample – Time-WIF and Time-FIW in corporate services

	TIME-WIF	TIME-FIW	
Mean	12.78	11.14	
Variance	2.23	1.98	
Observations	108	108	
Pooled Variance	2.12		
Hypothesized Mean Difference	0		
df	214		
t Stat	6.598		
P(T<=t) one-tail	0.01		

t Critical one-tail	1.76		
P(T<=t) two-tail	0.01		
t Critical two-tail	1.74		

Table: 66

t-Test: Two-Sample - Strain WIF and Strain FIW in corporate services

	STRAIN-WIF	STRAIN-FIW
Mean	12.010	10.896
Variance	2.226	2.415
Observations	108	108
Pooled Variance	2.293	
Hypothesized Mean Difference	0	
df	214	
t Stat	5.643	
P(T<=t) one-tail	0.01	
t Critical one-tail	1.891	
P(T<=t) two-tail	0.01	
t Critical two-tail	1.783	

ignou   Work –Life Balance among Women Professionals

Table: 67

t-Test: Two-Sample –Behavior WIF and Behavior FIW in corporate services

	BEHAVIOR-WIF	BEHAVIOR-FIW
Mean	9.289	9.645
Variance	2.220	2.285
Observations	108	108
Pooled Variance	2.265	
Hypothesized Mean Difference	0	
df	214	
t Stat	1.67	
P(T<=t) one-tail	0.154	
t Critical one-tail	1.77	
P(T<=t) two-tail	0.169	
t Critical two-tail	1.95	

Analysis along six dimensions showed difference between WIF and FIW along time, strain and but not in behaviour dimensions. Thus corporate services showed overall highest WLB score or 'conflict' as compared to other two sector. Within the sector, the dimensions along which imbalance was most prominently perceived were time, WIF, time-WIF and strain-WIF.

Table below shows the t –test evaluating the group means along the six dimensions for the academic sector.

ignou   Work –Life Balance among Women Professionals

Table: 68

t-Test: Two-Sample – Time-WIF and Time-FIW in academic sector

	TIME-WIF	TIME-FIW	
Mean	11.38	11.19	
Variance	2.29	1.78	
Observations	110	110	
Pooled Variance	2.14		
Hypothesized Mean Difference	0		
df	218		
t Stat	1.598		
P(T<=t) one-tail	0.33		
t Critical one-tail	1.86		
P(T<=t) two-tail	0.36		
t Critical two-tail	1.84		

Table: 69

t-Test: Two-Sample - Strain WIF and Strain FIW in academic sector

	STRAIN-WIF	STRAIN-FIW

ignou   Work –Life Balance among Women Professionals

Mean	11.001	10.866
Variance	2.226	2.415
Observations	110	110
Pooled Variance	2.293	
Hypothesized Mean Difference	0	
df	218	
t Stat	1.643	
P(T<=t) one-tail	0.41	
t Critical one-tail	1.711	
P(T<=t) two-tail	0.41	
t Critical two-tail	1.743	

Table: 70

t-Test: Two-Sample –Behavior WIF and Behavior FIW in academic sector

	BEHAVIOR-WIF	BEHAVIOR-FIW
Mean	9.826	9.131
Variance	2.411	2.302
Observations	110	110
Pooled Variance	2.345	
Hypothesized Mean Difference	0	

ignou   Work –Life Balance among Women Professionals

df	218	
t Stat	1.67	
P(T<=t) one-tail	0.154	
t Critical one-tail	1.87	
P(T<=t) two-tail	0.169	
t Critical two-tail	1.85	

There was no difference between dimensions along the six dimensional model, in the academic sector. Thus within the sector, the dimensions along which imbalance was most prominently perceived was time.

Similarly, responses in healthcare were evaluated on a six dimensional model.

Table: 71

t-Test: Two-Sample – Time-WIF and Time-FIW in healthcare sector

	TIME-WIF	TIME-FIW	
Mean	11.46	10.09	
Variance	2.12	1.96	
Observations	112	112	
Pooled Variance	2.08		
Hypothesized Mean Difference	0		

ignou   Work –Life Balance among Women Professionals

df	222		
t Stat	5.598		
P(T<=t) one-tail	0.01		
t Critical one-tail	1.86		
P(T<=t) two-tail	0.01		
t Critical two-tail	1.84		

Table: 72

t-Test: Two-Sample - Strain WIF and Strain FIW in healthcare sector

	STRAIN-WIF	STRAIN-FIW
Mean	11.161	10.496
Variance	2.126	2.315
Observations	112	112
Pooled Variance	2.223	
Hypothesized Mean Difference	0	
df	222	
t Stat	1.343	
P(T<=t) one-tail	0.11	
t Critical one-tail	1.611	
P(T<=t) two-tail	0.11	

ignou   Work –Life Balance among Women Professionals

t Critical two-tail	1.643	

Table: 73

t-Test: Two-Sample –Behavior WIF and Behavior FIW in healthcare sector

	BEHAVIOR-WIF	BEHAVIOR-FIW
Mean	9.926	9.431
Variance	2.211	2.202
Observations	112	112
Pooled Variance	2.205	
Hypothesized Mean Difference	0	
df	222	
t Stat	1.27	
P(T<=t) one-tail	0.174	
t Critical one-tail	1.47	
P(T<=t) two-tail	0.189	
t Critical two-tail	1.45	

There was a difference between dimensions along the six dimensional model, in the healthcare sector, with Time WIF showing greater WLB perception, along with time and WIF dimensions.

ignou   Work –Life Balance among Women Professionals

Thus overall order of imbalance was corporate services (IT/BPO/KPO)> Healthcare> Academic. The difference between all three sectors was statistically significant, with p< 0.05. Additionally, there was statistically significant difference between type of sector and dimensions along which WLB was perceived.

Table 74 enumerates the overall effect of independent variables on WLB along different dimensions.

Table: 74

Overall effect of independent variables on WLB dimensions

	Effect of dependent variable (WLB dimensions)		
Independent variable*	**Time, strain, behavior**	**WIF, FIW**	**Time-WIF, Time-FIW, Strain-WIF, Strain-FIW, Behavior WIF, Behavior FIW**
Years of experience	Negative correlation along Time, Strain	Negative correlation along WIF	Negative correlation along Time-WIF, Strain-WIF
Age	Negative correlation along Time, Strain	Negative correlation along WIF	Negative correlation along Time-WIF, Strain-WIF
Marital status	Imbalance or conflict more for married than unmarried		

ignou   Work –Life Balance among Women Professionals

Married (without children)	More 'imbalance' along Time	More 'imbalance' along WIF	More 'imbalance' along Time-WIF, Strain-WIF
Presence of children	More 'imbalance' along Time, Strain	More 'imbalance' along WIF, FIW	More 'imbalance' along Time-WIF, Time-FIW, Strain-WIF, Strain-FIW
Family support			
Instrumental support	Negative correlation along Time, Strain	Negative correlation along WIF, FIW	Negative correlation along Time WIF, Time FIW, Strain WIF, Strain FIW
Emotional support	-	-	Negative correlation along FIW dimension
Job involvement	Positive correlation along Time, Strain	-	Positive correlation along Time-WIF, Strain-WIF, Time FIW, Strain FIW
Type of sector			
Corporate services	More 'imbalance' along Time	More 'imbalance' along WIF	More 'imbalance' along Time-WIF, Strain-WIF
Academic	More	-	-

ignou   Work –Life Balance among Women Professionals

	'imbalance' along Time		
Healthcare	More 'imbalance' along Time	More 'imbalance' along WIF	More 'imbalance' along Time-WIF

*For discontinuous /categorical variables like marital status, presence of children, and type of sector, means were compared instead of correlation.

CHAPTER-5
DISCUSSION

DISCUSSION

This study set out to evaluate WLB experienced by respondents along its various dimensions, the difference along these dimensions. After evaluating WLB holistically along all six dimensions, it was considered as the dependent variable, and the relationships of independent variables like job involvement and family support was evaluated with respect to WLB along all dimensions. This section now evaluates the findings in greater depth, and tries to analyse the overall results achieved with respect to findings report in literature, by comparing and contrasting this research work's findings with literature findings. Subsequently, we attempt to understand what impact the data findings and their analysis have for the individual and the organizations, and how can these findings be applied and under what scenarios.

WLB- Six dimension model, and perception along different dimensions

Theorists also have started to notice the various types of work–family conflict (Netemeyer, Boles & McMurrian, 1996; Stephens & Sommer, 1993). In coherence with Greenhaus and Beutell's (1985) definition, three types of work–family conflict have been listed in theory: (a) time-based conflict, (b) strain-based conflict, and (c) behavior-based conflict. Time-based conflict may happen when time allotted to one role makes it tough to involve in the other role, strain-based conflict advises that strain felt in one role gets into and coincides with getting involved in the other role, and behavior-based conflict occurs when particular behaviors used in one role do not match with behavioral expectation in the other role (Greenhaus & Beutell, 1985). In 1991, Gutek et al. observed that each of these three types of work–family

ignou   Work –Life Balance among Women Professionals

conflict has two directions: (a) conflict due to work interfering with family (WIF) and (b) conflict due to family interfering with work (FIW). When these three types and two directions are put together six dimensions of work–family conflict result: (1) time-based WIF, (2) time-based FIW, (3) strain-based WIF, (4) strain-based FIW, (5) behavior-based WIF, and (6) behavior-based FIW.

To holistically study WLB, this research work has focused on all six dimensions/3 dimension-3 direction model. According to Carlson et al, the scale developed by them measures all six dimensions "using only 18 items". Additionally, the authors claimed, the scale allowed "each of the six dimensions to be examined." Thus scale developed by Carlson et al was used, and when considering WLB as a dependent variable, first step was to assess the responses along each of the six dimensions. Additionally, the dimensions are distinctive, and may not be mutually correlated. For example, in a study by Ejike Okonkwo, 2014, on Nigerian women, it was concluded that time-based work interference with family was not related to time-based family interference with work among women. Thus WIF and FIW being 2 distinctive dimensions, further support the 6 dimensional model, and need to evaluate response along each dimension separately.

Findings indicated that WLB perceived showed significant difference between time, strain and behaviour with 'imbalance' in time> strain> behaviour. Similarly imbalance or conflict was more along WIF as compared to FIW. In the six dimensional model, Time-WIF was the dimension along which, maximum conflict was perceived.

According to Parasuraman & Greenhaus,1997, time based conflict occurs "when the time demands of one role make it difficult or impossible to participate in another role". For example,

ignou   Work –Life Balance among Women Professionals

an urgent requirement at the job may coincide with a family function, resulting in the employee having to skip the latter. Strain based conflict occurs "when psychological from the demands of work or family role impacts the other role, making it difficult to fulfil the responsibilities of that role". For example, a person trying to meet sudden or heightened job related requirements, may be strained and may have to skip or delay responding to family needs

It is possible, based on this research's findings, that time dimension was the 'trigger point' for imbalance or conflict. This 'triggered' imbalance 'spilled over' the imbalance along strain dimension as well. Alternatively, strain dimension imbalance was triggered or perceived to a lesser extent, possibly due to individual specific moderating factors like coping skills etc. Since strain dimension WLB is mainly 'psychological form of conflict', individual specific moderating factors can reduce the impact. Similarly behaviour dimension conflict occurs "when the behaviours that are expected or appropriate in the family role are viewed as inappropriate or dysfunctional when used in the work role". Again behaviour modulation may reduce the impact along this dimension.

Thus it appeared that time conflict was getting triggered either earlier or tend to persist, due to conflicting job/family demands and/or limited effect of psychological coping or behaviour modulation on decreasing impact along time-dimension, since these do not change available time, or tasks at hand. Some of the stress from this dimension 'spilled' over to strain dimension, while behaviour dimension remained unaffected and related conflict was not perceived.

WLB- relationship with demographics

Years of experience

Crompton et al, 2005, in their cross cultural study examined national variations in reported levels of work-life conflict, drawing upon questions fielded in the 2002 Family module International Social Survey Programme (ISSP) surveys for Britain, France, Finland, Norway and Portugal. Their study included both men and women. They found that even though occupational class also had an influence on work-life conflict with professional/managerial employees having importantly greater work-life conflict than either middle level employees or manual employees, at the same time a relationship evaluation of work-life conflict by age implied that younger full-time employees had greater work-life conflict than old aged full-time workers(Pearson r = -0.044; p<0.01). It was not sure if similar middle level employees moved ahead to a higher managerial responsibility.

On the other hand, some researchers report that, individuals working in a managerial or higher status occupation report higher levels of conflict between work and their personal life. (Judge and Colquitt, 2004).

Since current research work dealt with different sectors, with varying level of entry age levels, age and years of experience were considered as separate independent variables. The average years of experience of respondents in the three sectors was 8.5-9 years.

There was a significant difference reported with WLB being highest in < 5years of experience group and 5-10 years of experience group as compared to other groups, and was most significant along time and strain dimension, and WIF direction. This corresponds with findings of Crompton et al, and Tausig et al, who have identified variables such as worker autonomy or life cycle to be linked to 'seniority' and influence WLB, but diverges from the findings of Judge et al, 2004 who reported higher imbalance in managerial roles. The latter research focused more

ignou   Work –Life Balance among Women Professionals

on occupational status or designation, than years per se. Additionally, Ahmad et.al (2003), found that fewer years of experience, negative family and friend support, and negative total work satisfaction were found to be significant predictors of psychological ill health among nurses. In addition, degree of satisfaction with family life was also found to be positively correlated with years of experience.

According to Tausig and Fenwick (2001), older adults report greater success with work-life balance. Lowe and Krahn (1988) found that young workers are less satisfied with their jobs in general than are older workers. Thus literature suggests difference in perception of life satisfaction between lesser experienced and more experienced respondents, with more experienced respondents being more satisfied with life, and better able to utilise coping to neutralise 'imbalance'.

Additionally, other work domain determinants such as job autonomy, and the existence of family-friendly work policies directly influence work-life balance (Jennings & McDougald, 2007). It seems likely that lesser experienced respondents may perceive less autonomy over jobs. Individuals with lower levels of perceived control, over their work are more likely to report high role overload and high interference between work and family roles (Baral and Bhargava, 2010).

Adjusting for life cycle differences like presence of children, reduced the difference further. Overall, it seemed that lesser experienced respondents, with lower perception of life satisfaction, lesser perception of job autonomy, and lesser 'coping' perceived greater 'imbalance' as compared to more experienced respondents, especially along time, strain and WIF dimensions.

Thus years of experience as an independent variable seemed to be negatively correlated with 'imbalance' Respondents in the <5 years of experience and 5-10 years of experience categories, showed greater 'imbalance' than more experienced respondents.

Age

Age as an independent variable as been evaluated with WLB with varying results reported. According to Crompton et al, and Hyman et al, increasing age is associated with lesser 'imbalance' possibly due to increased perception of family –life satisfaction among the respondents. However Rabl et al, 2009, reported age related 'stressor' to increase work family conflict.

Wang, Lawler & Shi, (2010) found that age and lifecycle determine and influence work life stress experienced by individuals. The newer generations have observed a shift in living style priorities resulting in making name sections. Those born after 1969, or the so called "Generation X", are reported to choose a living style that encompasses non-work time, inspite of other responsibilities, thus, may actively look for organizations who offer work-life balance programs Tausig and Fenwick (2001) found that old people have more success with work-life balance.

Current research work considered age to be a representative variable of life-stage/life-cycle. Among different models of life cycle, Roehling's model was considered in a simplified form.

The current research seeks to classify life-stage based on age as reflecting distinct career stages and in this way expand the research by moving the discussion beyond dependent children and working parents in order to encapsulate a broader definition of work–life balance as it applies to all employees. To this end four age groupings were presented and examined which represent distinct career stages. These stages were:

- Age 22-27, or early career stage;

- Age 28-33, or developing career stage;

- Age 34-39, or consolidating career stage

- Age 40+, represents advanced career stage.

The analysis showed significant difference in perceived WLB by different age groups. Thus 'imbalance' was perceived in the order 22-27 years age> 28-33 years of age> 34-39 years of age> 40+ years.

Not only were the differences significant, but the order of age groups in perceived WLB seemed to run parallel to findings in years of experience variable, suggesting overlap between the variables. These findings were in accordance with the findings of Wang et al, Tausig et al, and Maxwell et al. As with years of experience, different reasons including life-cycle related responsibilities, can account for this relationship. Adjusting for presence of children reduced the difference between age groups making it possible that factors like life satisfaction, coping, and perceived job autonomy may be the reason for increasing balance with age, or lower balance in age groups 22-27, and 28-33 years.

One more possible factor that influences WLB might be the variation of monetary safety vis-a-vis age. As per Reddy et al, 2010, "In Indian context, a lot of women, especially those from the lower middle class, are seeking the job market today because they have to augment the family income. They have to provide a better life for their families, pay their children's tuition fees and plan a better future for them." The theorists also found that "… it is seen that the women working due to financial needs reported higher WFC when compared to those working for other reasons."

While Crompton, Hyman have reported negative correlation between age and imbalance, Thriveni et al have reported positive correlation suggesting "As age progresses and women get married they will have more responsibilities at home to handle that affects their work life balance." However the latter study did not divide age into groups to assess deeper impact. Nor have too many researchers studied the correlation of age along directions and dimensions of WLB model.

Higgins et al. have tried to examine two of the dimensions, that is, WIF and FIW, in a study on both genders. They examined the impact of gender and life cycle stage on three components of work family conflict (i.e. role overload, interference from work to family and interference from family to work). The results indicated significant differences for gender and life cycle. Women reported experiencing significantly greater role overload than men. Again women were found to experience greater work to family interference than men. Interference was highest when the children were young, and lowest in families with older children. Going ahead, women found very prominent greater amounts of family interference with work as compared to men in initial years, but extent of interferences were at par with those of men"s in the third phase of life style (i.e. children 10 to 18 years).

The current research found that as with other independent variables, age as a demographic variable was found to be correlated with perceived WLB but the correlation was not equal across all dimensions and directions.

ignou   Work –Life Balance among Women Professionals

Age groups 34-39 and 40+ showed lesser imbalance, compared to younger age groups. The correlation was stronger along time and strain dimensions and WIF direction.

Although evaluating the causality was out of scope of this research, findings along different directions of WLB did seem to imply lack of sufficient time, as the major cause of WLB both with age and years of experience as the independent variables. This perceived 'time paucity' seemed to be greater in younger age groups and lesser experienced women professionals.

Lack of sufficient time, social and cultural norms as well as family responsibilities are the most significant challenges women face to achieve balance in their professional and personal life. Careful planning, organizing and allocating work are the most efficient ways women use to cope with challenging roles of work and family (Rehman, 2012)

It is possible these coping strategies evolve or improve with age or years of experience, leading to less perception of 'imbalance'.

There is also proof that there can be various pressures on a woman from her family and such pressures also are affected by the life stage of their children. According to Hamilton et al, 2006, those women with dependent kids go through more work-life imbalance than those females without dependent kids. In addition there may be organizational factors responsible for influencing relationship between age or years of experience and WLB. These include autonomy available, access to WLB policies, or organizational support.

Thus it is possible that a combination of various personal life factors like family responsibilities including children's responsibilities, family life cycle fluctuations and demands may influence age/years of experience and WLB correlation. In addition there may be individual

ignou   Work –Life Balance among Women Professionals

factors that may develop over a period of time, and with age, such as coping and time management.

Marital status

Martins, Eddleston & Veiga, (2002) found married individuals to give more emphasis to their personal lives than their single counterparts. The reason could be the former experiencing a lack of separation or difficulty keeping separation between work and home boundaries (Hall & Richter, 1988), which can negatively influence both work and family life. Md-Sidin, et al. (2008) reported that individuals who are married experience more work-life conflict than those who are unmarried.

As per Boise et al, having greater amounts of family pressures lead to high time pressures and stress on the family, and this clashes with the person's role at work. Pressures from both roles and what husbands expect from their working wives was prominently linked to more WFC and FWC in the respondents in the current research. Sharma, (1999) reported that the help and engagement of one's husband positively links to less levels of role conflict come across by married working females. Carlson et al. reported that facing pressures from work negatively impacted family responsibilities in more examples as compared to family demands that affected work responsibilities.

Agarwal et al found that there are more factors that affect married women and since they have domestic responsibilities (from which married men usually escape) so they leave on time. To have a sufficient support system for children is a primary issue for women. Because of these setbacks, when there is stress from work or an important timeline to meet, women usually could not deliver by their male colleagues for being unavailable or not pulling their weight in the

ignou   Work –Life Balance among Women Professionals

team; the perceived unwillingness of women to put in the required work in such a high pressure job produces resentment and a tendency to marginalize women in terms of allotment of work. This leads to work environment stress leading to work-life conflict. Role overload, depended care issues quality of health, problems in time management and lack of proper social support are the major factors influencing work life balance women employees in India (Mathew and Panchanatham, 2011).

Thus most of the studies have reported a positive correlation between marital status and 'imbalance'. However, Higgins et al. found that family involvement and family expectations were related to conflict in the family, but not related to WFC.

The present research work revealed significant association between marital status and perceived WLB. Married respondents reported more conflict or imbalance as compared to unmarried women. This is in agreement with Martine et al, Hall et al, Md-Sidin et al, Sharma et al and Agarwal et al, but at variance with Higgins et al.

Since boundaries of both family and work are permeable, role stereotyping, role overload and expectations of dependents care, may be contributing to the perceived imbalance among the respondents. It is generally women who take the primary responsibility for childcare and who, in situations of conflict, adjust their working lives to accommodate family pressures (Falkenberg and Monachello, 1990; Ramu, 1989). All this puts an extra pressure on women employees, triggering imbalance along time and strain dimensions, since these are les amenable to behavioural modulation.

According to Agarwal, 2014, when a woman achieves a successful work-life balance, she has job satisfaction and becomes highly committed and productive and succeeds in her career.

But, in certain cases women may not be able to succeed due to inability in balancing their work and personal life. They may be unable to set their priorities. As a result they withdraw from work due to simple reasons like taking care of her children, aged in laws/parents, and other family pressures. If the spouse is able to share some of their responsibilities, success and representation at work may increase.

Presence of children

The presence or absence of children in the family continues to make a significant difference in the degree of balance that individuals experience (Tausig & Fenwick, 2001). Parental status has been found to be a determinant of parents placing increased importance on the role of family (Blau, et al., 1998). Family responsibilities such as household time demands, family responsibility level, household income, spousal support and life course stage have been found to be sources of work-life stress (Jennings & McDougald, 2007).

Dual earner couples with no children report greater work-life balance, while both single and married parents report significantly lower levels of perceived balance compared to single, non-parents (Tausig & Fenwick). According to Agarwal et al, in a high-pressure job, women with young children often find it difficult to cope and end up leaving employment. Women also often find it difficult to make up for the loss of experience and learning during this period, and maternity leave can cause a major setback to their career growth and personal development. Young couples employ various strategies to manage their domestic situation, from heavy dependence on servants and crèches, to reconstituting the joint family by inviting one or the other set of parents to live with them, primarily to provide childcare. But making and maintaining these arrangements often only add to the stress on women.

As children and elderly family members require additional care, the obligation to meet their needs can influence family roles, which can create inter-role conflict and impact family roles, producing FWC. Studies also reported that women having younger children experience more role conflicts.(Khan et al, Beutell et al). Additionally, not only is childcare often a common reason for asking for 'work-from-home' by women, according to a recent research from Furman University on 650 participants, such requests are likely to be granted only to 57% of women employees as compared to 70% of men. Also, women seeking WLB were viewed more negatively than men.

In this research work, in terms of dimensions affected, presence of children had a greater association or impact on WLB than all other demographic variables. Presence of children made respondents experience conflict/ imbalance, especially along time dimension, strain dimension and WIF dimensions.

This is in line with most of the research literature like Trausig et al, Jennings et al, Agarwal et a, Boise et al, Khan et al, Beutell et al, but at variance with Higgins et al.

Thus similar to marital status, presence of children increases the work-family spillover and conflict. This is due to pressure of dual role, management of dependents and at the same time performing at job, and role stereotyping especially in Indian culture, resulting in working mothers shouldering most of the household responsibilities. In the breadwinner versus homemaker stereotyping, that is still prevalent in Indian culture for men and women, role of mother or maternal responsibilities are 'least negotiable'. Hence presence of children more significantly impacts WLB than other demographic variables in this study.

Job involvement

Among the non- demographic independent variables considered in this research work, first one was Job involvement (JI). Kanungo's (1982) definition was adopted for this study. Kanungo described job involvement as a "generalized cognitive state of psychological identification with the individual's cognition about his or her identification with work and strong support of the self-image definition of job involvement." According to Kanungo et al, earlier conceptualizations of job involvement have failed to distinguish two different contexts in which an individual can show personal involvement (Kanungo, 1981). The two contexts are (a) specific or particular job context and (b) generalized work context. Involvement in a specific job is not the same as involvement with work in general. The former is a belief descriptive of the present job and tends to be a function of how much the job can satisfy one's present needs. But involvement with work in general or the centrality of work in one's life is a belief about the value of general work in one's life, and it is more a function of one's past cultural conditioning or socialization. Thus to focus on specific type of jobs, across various sectors, in a common culture, job involvement is more relevant than work involvement. Hence former was used in this research.

Organizational effectiveness and productivity can be affected by Job involvement, making it an important attitudinal variable that impacts work (Seo,2013). Organizations may be significantly benefited by employees showing high levels of job involvement (Diefendorff, 2002). Thus, Job involvement may be linked with or affect work performance, efficiency and behavior (Yang, 2006)

Some researchers report that since Job involvement influences the amount of energy and time invested on work, it may lead to conflict between work and family roles (Frone et al., 1992). Greenhaus et al. (1989) reported that job involvement increased the work-family conflict along the time-based and strain–based dimensions among women. According to them, the reason for this was the requirement of high levels of psychological involvement which in turn led to increased energy and time being devoted to job, resulting in WFC. Thus, job involvement is reported to be positively correlated with time commitment to work and negatively correlated to time commitment to family.

Interference between work and non-work responsibilities has a number of negative outcomes that have been well established in the literature. In terms of job attitudes, employees reporting high levels of both work-to-life and life-to-work conflict tend to exhibit lower levels of job satisfaction and organizational commitment (Burke & Greenglass, 1999; Kossek & Ozeki, 1998). Behavioural outcomes of both directions of conflict include reduced work effort, reduced performance, and increased absenteeism and turnover (Frone, Yardley, & Markel, 1997; Greenhaus, Collins, Singh, & Parasuraman, 1997). Both work-to-life and life-to-work conflict have also been associated with increased stress and burnout (Anderson et al., 2002) cognitive difficulties such as staying awake, lack of concentration, and low alertness (MacEwen & Barling, 1994), and reduced levels of general health and energy (Frone, 1996). While the majority of work-life balance research focuses on employees' family responsibilities, there are also a number of studies that recognize commitments to friends and community groups, expanding the affected population to virtually all employees (e.g., Beauregard, 2006; Tausig & Fenwick, 2001). The implications for organizations are clear: work-life conflict can have negative repercussions for employee performance.

The present research work found a moderate positive correlation between 'imbalance' or conflict and job involvement along the time and strain dimensions. There was mild positive correlation along WIF and FIW dimensions, but the difference was not significant.

Findings are in agreement with those reported bu Frone et al, Greenhaus et al, and partially agree with the findings of Williams et al.

Williams and Alliger (1994) found that spillover of unpleasant moods occur both from work to family settings and from family to work though evidence for the spillover of pleasant moods was weak. Both family to work and work to family spillovers were stronger for women than men. Further, it was found that extent to which work interfered with family for a given day was found to be positively related to self reported job involvement for that day. Extent to which family interfered with work on a given day was found to be positively related to distress in family roles during the day, family intrusion into work during the day and self reported family involvement for that day. Thus according to them WIF was positively correlated with JI and FIW was positively correlated with FI (Family involvement). Since this study was on both genders, it is possible that subgroup analysis on women alone (similar to present research) may report slightly different results.

Aryee and Luk (1996) in a study of 207 dual earner couples in Hong Kong found that men significantly identified more with the work role, had more experience in the workforce, and perceived more spouse support. In contrast, women significantly, identified more with the family role, had main responsibility for childcare, spent more time per week with the children and perceived more need for family responsive policies. In addition, the results revealed that women balance their work and family identity by trading off one for the other. In contrast, men are able to simultaneously identify with work and family roles.

Thus, for women, it appears to be a trade-off between involvement in job and family domains, and enhanced involvement at job may lead to conflict because family responsibilities do not proportionally decrease to take some burden off.

Family Support

Social support can include family and work place support especially managerial support. Managerial support has been reported to play an important role in organizational effectiveness. Managers are seen by employees, as representatives of the organization who evaluate their performance and report to higher level management. Due to this perception, employees see the support from their managers as organizational support. (Eisenberger, 2002).

Family support has been less discussed in research area on job involvement, and has two components, that is, instrumental support, which refers to tangible help from the partner in the form of participation in home maintenance and child care; and information or emotional support, which refers to information, advice, affirmation of affection, and concern for the receiver's welfare displayed by the partner (Parasuraman & Greenhaus, 1994).

According to Parasuraman, 1996, high levels of instrumental support provided by one's partner can ease the burden of family-role demands, and lead to lesser family-work conflict. They also report positive correlation between spouse support and time spent with family, perhaps due to reciprocity. Suchet and Barling (1986) in a study of interrole conflict, spouse support and marital functioning found that support from one's husband may assist employed mothers cope with their own interrole conflict, as husbands' supportive behaviour and attitude might help in reducing the opposing role demands on, and unrealistic role expectations of employed mothers.

On the other hand, Loerch et al. (1989) examined the relationships among family domain variables and three sources of work family conflict (time, strain and behaviour based) for both men and women. Family domain variables examined included time based (number of children, spouse work hours per week, couple's employment status) strain based (conflict within family, spouse support, quality of experience in spouse or parent role) and behaviour based antecedents, family intrusions (parental, marital, home responsibilities) and role involvement. The results indicated that the time based antecedents (number of children, spouse work hours, couple's employment status) were not significantly related to any form of work family conflict for men or women. Strain based antecedent, conflict within family, was found to have a positive relationship with work family conflict. However, the negative relationship of other strain based antecedents (spouse support, quality of spouse and parental experiences) and work family conflict was not supported. The behaviour based antecedent, role congruity, was not significantly related to any form of work family conflict. Thus according to them, spouse support did not decrease conflict.

Adams et al. (1996) developed and tested a model of the relationship between work and family. The results suggested that higher levels of family emotional and instrumental support were associated with lower levels of family interfering with work. Frone et al. (1997) reported that family related support (spouse & other family members) may reduce family to work conflict by reducing family distress and parental overload. Aryee et al. (1999b) examined the relationship between role stressors, interrole conflict, and well-being and the moderating influences of spousal support and coping behaviours among a sample of Hong Kong Chinese employed parents in dual-earner families (N=243) and found that role stressors (work overload and parental overload) and spousal support set significantly explained the variance in both work family conflict (WFC) and family work conflict (FWC). Spousal support was found to be a negative predictor of WFC while parental overload was a positive predictor. Spousal support was found to moderate the effect of parental overload on FWC. FWC was negatively related to job and life satisfaction, but neither WFC nor FWC was related to family satisfaction.

Thus evidence from literature suggested that higher the parental pressure, higher is the work family conflict and higher the spouse support, lower is the work family conflict. However, most studies except Adams et al, considered family support to be a single variable, without components emotional and instrumental support.

Present research work evaluated the correlation of overall FS and emotional and instrumental support. Findings suggest a moderate negative correlation between instrumental support and conflict and between overall support and conflict. While relation between emotional support and conflict was mild. The negative correlation was along time, strain and FIW dimensions. These findings partially support Adams et al, and for overall family support, are consistent with Frone et al, Aryee et al and Parasuraman et al, while vary with findings reported by Loerch et al. Thus it is apparent that what most negates the conflict is the instrumental support from spouse or family members. In other words, getting things done at household level makes greater impact than emotional support. This also explains the overall perceived 'imbalance' by respondents along time dimension- that is, behaviour modulation (behavioural dimension) or psychological coping (strain dimension) do not help with household chores which women are expected to burden alone, most of the time. This results in residual conflict along time dimension which responds most to instrumental support. This support may also reduce the trade-off between job and family involvement less, and increase overall involvement.

Type of sector

Sectors are related to the type of work undertaken. There is evidence in literature that type of work, work characteristics, and expectations influence work family conflict. In earlier times, attaining work-life balance was considered the sole responsibility of the employee, not the employer (Bailyn, 1993). As compared to these historic times, the recent 21st century trend makes it necessary for institutions of higher education to adopt meaningful work life policies. (Bailyn 1993; Wiliams, 2000)

Researchers have reinforced the existence of WLB problems for employers in the corporate world. Matos and Galinsky (2011) analyzed data from the National Study of the Changing Workforce and the National Study of Employers, They considered sectors like health services; hospitality, restaurant, and tourism; manufacturing; and retail. They found that the majority of employees, 60-69%,reported that they lacked time for themselves and for their spouses/partners. Researchers also found that employees who were employed in flexible work environments reported that they had greater amounts of time to spend with their spouses/partners and children.

Research by Friedman and Greenhaus (2000) substantiates this finding; they surveyed employed business school alumni from two institutions in an attempt to investigate the relationship between work and home for corporate employees. Respondents, particularly those who were parents, reported a lack of time for family. Those who worked for employers that they identified as family-friendly, however, reported lower levels of conflict between their personal and professional lives. Friedman and Greenhaus concluded that support at home and family friendly workplaces can help to ease work-life integration.

ignou   Work –Life Balance among Women Professionals

Quantitative and qualitative research has documented that work-life balance is problematic for corporate employees. However, work-life balance research on the corporate workplace, as depicted in the preceding studies, often draws conclusions from studies of employees across different industries.

Many researchers like Finkel, Olswang and She 1994; Grant et al, 2000; Ward and Wolf-Wendel, 2005, have reported that many academicians and faculty members fear to avail work-life policies to save their reputation as a scholar. Thus while organizational policies may help they are often not availed.

While such research offers insight into broad workplace trends, Anderson, Morgan, and Wilson (2002) noted that we know little about the work-life experiences of employees by industry. Varied organizational cultures exist across industries. Thus, employees in different industries may experience different work-life balance problems. (Anderson et al., 2002).

Butler et al. (2005) surveyed 91 parents employed in non-professional occupations for 14 days about their job characteristics and work family conflict. Results showed that there was significant daily variation in work to family conflict (WFC) and work to family facilitation (WFF) that was predictable from daily job characteristics. Greater daily demands were associated with increase in daily levels of WFC and higher levels of daily control at work were associated with decrease in daily levels of WFC.

Drew and Murtagh (2005) examined the experience and attitude of female and male senior managers towards work life balance. The study was undertaken in a major Irish organization, for which work life balance was a strategic corporate objective. The finding of the

ignou   Work –Life Balance among Women Professionals

study was that greatest obstacle to achieving work life balance was the "long hours" culture, in which availing oneself of flexible options (e.g. flextime/working from home) is incompatible with holding a senior management post. Alam et al. (2009) explored the correlation between working hours and work family imbalance, for three focused groups, namely, teaching professionals and two groups from corporate houses. It was found that respondents working for 5-7 hours a day did not consider working hours as a factor to affect work and family balance. On the other hand, women managers in corporate sector, having long working hours (9-10 hours a day) agreed that time was a crucial factor for work family imbalance. The study approved the association between working hour and work family conflict. 99 per cent of women managers reported to have work family conflict because of 9 -10 hours work everyday. While only 20 per cent involved in teaching reported so.

Sandhu and Mehta (2006) in a study of 271 women working in service sector in Punjab found that gender role attitude and spillover between work and family roles was the most important factor that affected the career of these women. It was also found that nature of organization and education had a significant impact on work family conflict. Pal and Saksvik (2008) in a cross cultural study of 27 doctors and 328 nurses from Norway and 111 doctors and 136 nurses from India, found that predictors of job stress were different for doctors and nurses in India and Norway. In the case of Norwegian nurses, work family conflict was one of the predictors of job stress while in the case of Indian nurses high family work conflict was one of the predictors of job stress.

Galinsky and Johnson (1998) found that having a larger proportion of top executive positions filled by women was associated with greater provision of work life balance policies. They also found that companies with a larger proportion of women in them workforce were more

ignou   Work –Life Balance among Women Professionals

likely to invest in policies such as job sharing, part time work, flexible time off policies and child care. It was further observed that companies employing greater proportion of hourly workers, people who are generally concentrated in lower paid jobs, were least likely to offer work life balance policies.

Rajadhyaksha and Smita (2004) examined work and family research in the Indian context from independence till mid 2000. According to them, work and family research in India appeared to have followed two separate and disconnected paths. Women study centres focused on rural and underprivileged women while the other psychosocial researchers examined work and family relations within urban setting and there has been little cross pollination between the two streams. Major conclusions drawn included: After independence, the government and/or organizational policies appeared to be in favour of working men rather than working women and were more in nature of welfare measures for the worker and his family. During mid 1970s to mid 1980s, plight of working women (especially underprivileged) was deteriorating and nature of family organization was contributing to their deprivation, and at the same time, the picture of urban educated women was emerging. During mid 1980s to mid 1990s gender differences in work and family research were examined. Working status was not a guarantee of equitable relationships within the family. In the mid 1990s to 2000 liberalization impacted the work family research. Organizations in the new economy sectors (e.g. IT and ITES industry) started family friendly measures, more as an imitation of western organizational practices than as a felt need to help employees balance their work and life.

Wesley and Muthuswamy (2005) in a study of 230 teachers in an engineering college in Coimbatore, India, found that work to family conflict was more common than

ignou   Work –Life Balance among Women Professionals

family to work conflict, thus indicating that permeability of work into family was more than permeability of family into work.

Thus overall literature suggests variations in the levels of WLB experienced by employees in different sectors, due to various organization specific or individual specific variables, policies and utilisation of those policies.

Present research work also suggested inter sectoral variations. Respondents from all three sectors reported some conflict or imbalance in time dimension, with corporate services also reporting imbalance in strain and WIF dimensions. Overall order of imbalance was corporate services > healthcare > academic, however imbalance was reported by all three sectors.

This can be due to various factors. There is a perception linking daily hours put by a employee to career progression, especially in corporate services. Additionally, evidence from literature suggests work spill over resulting in overstay, in all three sectors. Also, in a developing country like India, WLB policies are often non-existent or exist only to match up to global organizations, but may not be implemented in spirit. Besides, women face additional problems of perception when they try to avail WLB policy benefits as compared to men, and are more likely to be declined by their managers. Thus despite sectoral differences, the commonality that al 3 sectors reported some imbalance or conflict in time dimension, suggests that WLB as a concept and an important influence affecting employee output, still remains a 'work in progress' in developing economy like India. Different barriers or constraints in different domains, like WLB policies and implementation, working hour spillover, perception disadvantages, perception of job autonomy etc need to be overcome either simultaneously or at least in a phased manner, to buffer negative impact of work on life.

Summary:

This chapter discussed findings in light of existing research and hypotheses. Independent variables affect WLB differentially along various dimensions. A dimension most affected is the time dimension, which may be a triggering dimension. Instrumental support is a major alleviating variable for conflict, while presence of children increases conflict along most dimensions.

CHAPTER -6

IMPLICATIONS, LIMITATIONS AND DIRECTIONS FOR FUTURE RESEARCH

Findings, Implications, Limitations and Directions for Future Research

Findings

This research work has extended prior research work on WLB in several important ways. To holistically study WLB, this research work has focused on all six dimensions/3 dimension-3 direction model.

Findings indicated that WLB perceived showed significant difference between time, strain and behaviour with 'imbalance' in time> strain> behaviour. Similarly imbalance or conflict was more along WIF as compared to FIW. In the six dimensional model, Time-WIF was the dimension along which, maximum conflict was perceived. Thus it appeared that time conflict was getting triggered either earlier or tend to persist, resulting in some of the stress from this dimension being 'spilled' over to strain dimension, while behaviour dimension remained unaffected and related conflict was not perceived.

Among demographic variables, since current research work dealt with different sectors, with varying level of entry age levels, age and years of experience were considered as separate independent variables. The average years of experience of respondents in the three sectors was 8.5-9 years. After adjusting for presence of children, imbalance was highest in < 5years of experience group and 5-10 years of experience group as compared to other groups, and was most significant along time and strain dimension, and WIF direction. Overall, it seemed that lesser experienced respondents, with lower perception of life satisfaction, lesser perception of job autonomy, and lesser 'coping' perceived greater 'imbalance' as compared to more experienced respondents, especially along time, strain and WIF dimensions.

Current research work considered age to be a representative variable of life-stage/life-cycle. The analysis showed significant difference in perceived WLB by different age groups. Thus 'imbalance' was perceived in the order 22-27 years age> 28-33 years of age> 34-39 years of age> 40+ years. Like with age, adjusting for presence of children reduced the difference between age groups making it possible that factors like life satisfaction, coping, and perceived job autonomy may be the reason for increasing balance with age, or lower balance in age groups 22-27, and 28-33 years. Another probable factor impacting WLB may be difference in financial security with respect to age.

Other demographic variable evaluated in this research was marital status. Findings revealed significant correlation between marital status and perceived WLB. Married respondents reported more conflict or imbalance as compared to unmarried women. Since boundaries of both family and work are permeable, role stereotyping, role overload and expectations of dependents care, may be contributing to the perceived imbalance among the respondents. It is generally women who take the primary responsibility for childcare and who, in situations of conflict, adjust their working lives to accommodate family pressures triggering imbalance along time and strain dimensions.

In this research work, presence of children had a greater correlation with WLB than all other demographic variables. Presence of children had a moderately positive correlation with conflict/

imbalance, especially along time dimension. There was also mild positive correlation with imbalance along strain and WIF dimensions. Presence of children increases the work-family spillover and conflict. This is due to pressure of dual role, management of dependents and at the same time performing at job, and role stereotyping especially in Indian culture, resulting in working mothers shouldering most of the household responsibilities.

Among the non- demographic independent variables considered in this research work, first one was Job involvement. The present research work found a moderate positive correlation between 'imbalance' or conflict and job involvement along the time and strain dimensions. For women, it appears that involvement in job and family domains are conflicting, and increased involvement at job may lead to conflict because family responsibilities do not proportionally decrease to take some burden off.

Second non-demographic variable considered was family support. Present research work evaluated the correlation of overall FS and emotional and instrumental support. Findings suggest a moderate negative correlation between instrumental support and conflict and between overall support and conflict. While relation between emotional support and conflict was mild. Thus it is apparent that what most negates the conflict is the instrumental support from spouse or family members.

Similarly, sectoral analysis suggested that all sectors reported conflict along time dimension, while corporate service also reported imbalance along strain and WIF dimensions. This might be related to inadequate presence or uptake of WLB policies in india, perception disadvantage for women, and time spillover with varying degree of flexibility and job autonomy.

Implications

For Individual

At individual level time dimension appears to be the key dimension triggering WLB. There is little that behavioural modulation or psychological coping can do to buffer time dimension imbalance.

It is likely that, in Indian context, a woman's family domain is more permeable and less flexible. Thus work tends to easily spill over into family domain (WIF), and lack of flexibility in family domain leads to conflict. This is especially evident it one attempts to link the findings of this research work. Since **most conflict is experienced in time dimension, WIF direction, across all sectors and is most aggravated by marriage and presence of children, and most negated by instrumental support, it appears that for an individual gender based stereotypes, family expectations and shouldering of responsibilities on both domains simultaneously, lead to conflict.**

Strategies directed at both work place and home, may be needed to reduce the conflict. On the professional front, women need to assert themselves professionally and make an effort in updating knowledge, skills and enhance their perceived value. This in turn should lead to improved outlook and them being taken seriously if, due to unmitigable circumstances, they do

ignou   Work –Life Balance among Women Professionals

need to avail WLB policies. Thus 'perception deficit' needs to be overcome- perhaps assertiveness and self progression through skill enhancement is an important step towards that goal.

On personal front, outsourcing some of the household chores, and not comparing oneself with a housewife, may make life simpler. Thus labor role or labor division in family domain seems to be a possible solution to women across sectors in India, who report experiencing work life imbalance.

For Organization

There is also a strong business case in support of work-life balance. Evidence from independent research as well as from employers' own assessments of flexible working practices shows that helping staff to strike a balance between paid work and personal life can lead to improved recruitment and retention, reduction of absenteeism, and an improved staff commitment and productivity.

For companies to remain competitive, it's critical they attract and keep the best employees. Current research work has shown that spillover is mostly from work to family, and in time dimension, is present in all sectors. Thus organizations need to evolve WLB policies that take Indian cultural requirements into consideration, especially role stereotyping faced by women.

Additionally they need to ensure policy utilisation is not perceived as a sign of 'weakness' rather a helping tool that can, if adequately supported by senior management, enhance work output and reduce role related stress. Perhaps managerial support in form of work structuring, limiting time spillover, and thoughtful, gender neutral response to request for availing WLB policies,, can act like organisational 'instrumental support' and buffer the impact of imbalance or help in striking balance.

Organizations can help out women by offering supervisor support and WLB policies, thus avoiding burnout and separation of the committed employees. More than conceiving initiatives for WLB, it is important that availing these initiatives is encouraged to employees who have a genuine need, and have overall shown progress. Supervisors can also play a role is ensuring male colleagues do not look down upon their women co-workers, and sharing and team working is encouraged. The supervisor's understanding and unbiased perception will act as 'instrumental support' and buffer the conflict.

Giving women opportunities to balance work and life, is not only productive for the company but also leads to better gender diversity at all levels including at senior level, which in turn would benefit the employees by increasing the take up of WLB policies, and benefit employer by increasing output. The business case for including women in companies has been made and emphasised time and again. However, there are still too few female directors on the boards of Indian companies. India ranks at the bottom in the overall proportion of men to women in the workplace. In a country where most of the employed women are still part of the unorganised sector, women in senior management in formal sectors like IT/ BPO can drive, enable and transform the female participation. And this inclusivity will lead to better perception of female co-workers among male colleagues, better framing take up of WLB policies, lesser burnout and attrition, and better economic output for the organization.

Limitations

Since the responses were mainly self reported there was a chance of common method bias or variance due to measurement method rather than constructs themselves. However, according to Spector (1987), concerns over common method bias are usually unsubstantiated. Additionally, self reporting format was unavoidable since only respondents themselves know about the imbalance they are facing or support they are getting.

Another limitation is that findings of three sectors may not be applicable across other sectors as nature and type of job and working hours vary from sector to sector.

There are other variables that may influence the impact of WLB perceived by respondents, such as encouragement by HR to avail WLB policies, supervisor's gender, life cycle status and past experience on WLB etc. It is possible that some of these factors may influence responses from respondents, but overall findings reveal that a generalised conclusion can be drawn about conflict perceived by respondents.

Similarly, respondents with similar skills and experience, may have different education levels and type of education. While education does impact an individual's mindset, this research mainly concentrates on existing job and family conditions, across various dimensions to understand WLB. Understanding if past experiences in education or upbringing had any impact on present perceptions was out of scope of current research. This work has concentrated on respondents' perception of conflict at a particular time, and different respondents together formed different stages of life, to give an idea of time-cycle or life-cycle based WLB perceived in domains of post-education work, and family life.

Future research

Every study leaves scope for further research. Based on the findings of the study certain areas for further research were identified.

1. It was observed that time dimension was the one subscale that got highest score when measuring conflict. Further research can be to find out what are the factors at individual level and organizational level that mainly influence and affect time dimension

2. Age group of children was not considered in this study, perhaps it is a variable that may impact WLB since presence of children was found to be correlated with conflict. A more detailed evaluation of children at different age-groups and their impact on WLB needs to be considered.

3. While WLB policies may impact and buffer conflict, studies don't report its impact in a dimension-wise manner. It needs to be evaluated if policies themselves or their uptake impact WLB along time dimension.

4. Instrumental support from family members is an important factor in reducing conflict. It is possible that instrumental support at work place has a synergistic effect with instrumental support from family. Thus this needs further evaluation.

5. Factors like spouse' occupation, financial status and type of family were out of scope of current study. They need to be evaluated in a direction-wise manner with respect to WLB to assess their effect of conflict.

6. While time seemed to be the most affected dimension, it is unclear if there is a cause and effect or sequential impact among the dimensions of WLB. For example, it is possible that time dimension gets affected earlier and in a sequential manner it impacts first strain and then behaviour. This needs to be considered in depth.

Conclusion

Current research work highlights the importance of work life balance, and perception of imbalance in women workers. Respondents across all three sectors-corporate service, healthcare, academic, perceived some degree of conflict between work and family domains. Additionally, they reported to be pressurised along the time dimension. Since previous research works have highlighted increasing imbalance in recent times, it is important to search for factors that can buffer the perception of conflict. One such important factor unearthed by this research was instrumental support from family members. When linked with factor correlated with most imbalance- presence of children, it is clear that support from spouse in getting household chores done, can go a long way in reducing the conflict, make family domain more flexible and less permeable.

REFERENCES

References

Adams, G. A., King, L. A., & King, D. W. (1996). Relationships of job and family involvement, family social support, and work–family conflict with job and life satisfaction. *Journal of applied psychology, 81*(4), 411.

Agarwal, P. (2014). A Study of Work Life Balance with Special Reference to Indian Call Center Employees. *International Journal of Engineering and Management Research, 4*(1), 157-164.

Ahmad, S., & Skitmore, M. (2003). Work-family conflict: A survey of Singaporean workers. *Singapore Management Review, 25*(1), 35-52.

Alam, S. S., Jani, M. F. M., & Omar, N. A. (2011). An empirical study of success factors of women entrepreneurs in southern region in Malaysia. *International Journal of Economics and Finance, 3*(2), 166

Allen, T. D. (2001). Family-supportive Work Environments: The Role of Organizational Perceptions. *Journal of Vocational Behavior, 58*, 414-435.

Allen, T. D., Herst, D. E. L., Bruck, C. S., & Sutton, M. (2000). Consequences associated with work-to-family conflict: A review and agenda for future research. Journal of Occupational Health Psychology, 5, 278–308.

Altucher, K., & Williams, L. (2003). Family clocks: Timing parenthood. In P. Moen (Ed.),
It's about time: Couples and careers (pp. 49–59). Ithaca, NY: Cornell University
Press.

Alexandris, K., Tsorbatzoudis, C. & Grouios, G. (2002). Perceived constraints on recreational
sport participation: Investigating their relationship with intrinsic motivation, extrinsic
motivation and amotivation. *Journal of Leisure Research, 34* (3), 233-252.

Anderson, D. M., Morgan, B. L., & Wilson, 1. B. (2002). Perceptions of family-friendly
policies: university versus corporate employees. *Journal of Family and Economic Issues,*
23(1), 73-92.

Anderson, S. E., Coffey, B. S., & Byerly, R. T. (2002). Formal organizational initiatives and
informal workplace practices: Links to work-family conflict and job-related outcomes.
Journal of Management, 28(6): 787-810.

Andreassi, J.K. & Thompson, C.A. (2008). Work-family culture: Current research and future
directions. In Korabik, Lero, & Whitehead (Eds): Handbook of Work-Family Integration.
Research, theory, and best practices. New York: Elsevier.

Aryee, S., & Luk, V. (1996). Balancing lwo Major Parts of Adult Life Experience: Work and
Family Identity Among Dual-Earner Couples. *Human Relations, 49*(4), 465-487.

ignou   Work –Life Balance among Women Professionals

Ashforth, B. E., Kreiner, G. E., & Fugate, M. (2000). All in a day's work: Boundaries and micro role transitions. *Academy of Management Review, 25*, 472-491

Bacharach, S., Bamberger, P. & Conley, S. (1991). Work-home conflict among nurses and engineers: Mediating the impact of role stress on burnout and satisfaction at work. *Journal of Organizational Behaviour, 12*, 39-53.

Bailyn, L. (1993). Breaking the mold: Women, men, and time in the new corporate world. New York, NY: The Free Press.

Bailyn, L., Drago, R., & Kochan, T. (2001). Integrating work andfamily life: A holistic approach. Cambridge, MA: MIT, Sloan School of Management.

Baral, R. & Bhargava, S. (2010). Work-family enrichment as a mediator between organizational interventions for work-life balance and job outcomes. *Journal of Managerial Psychology, 25* (3), 274-300.

Barnett, R. C. & Hyde, 1. S. (2001). Women, men, work, and family. *American Psychologist, 56*(10), 781-796.

Barnett, R. (2002, April 11). Role stress/strain and work-family, a sloan work and family encyclopedia entry. Sloan Work and Family Research Network

Barnett, R. C. (2004). Women and multiple roles: Myths and reality. Harvard Review Psychiatry, 12(3), 158-164.

Barnett, K. A., Del Campo, R. L., Del Campo, D. S., & Steiner, R. L. (2003). Work and family balance among dual-earner working-class Mexican-Americans: Implications for therapists. Contemporary Family Therapy, 25(4), 353-366.

Barnett, R. C. (1998). Toward a review and reconceptualization of the work/family literature. *Genetic, Social, and General Psychology Monographs,* 124(2), 125-182.

Bekker, M., Willemse, J. & De Goeij, J. (2010). The role of individual differences in particular autonomy-connectedness in women"s and men"s work-family balance. *Women & Health, 50,* 241-261

Bell, A. S., Rajendran, D., & Theiler, S. (2012). Job stress, wellbeing, work-life balance and work-life conflict among Australian academics. *Sensoria: A Journal of Mind, Brain & Culture, 8*(1), 25-37.

Bellavia. G., & Frone, M. (2005). Work-family conflict. In J. Barling, E. K. Kelloway, & M. Frone (Eds.), *Handbook of Work Stress,* (pp.113-147). Sage Publications

Beauregard, T. A. & Henry, L. C. (2009). Making the link between work-life balance practices and organizational performance. *Human Resource Management Review,* 19, 9-22.

Behson, S. J. (2002). The relative contribution of formal and informal organizational work family support. *Journal of Vocational Behavior, 66*(3), 487-500.

Beutell, N. J., & Greenhaus, J. H. (1983). Integration of home and nonhome roles: Women's conflict and coping behavior. *Journal of Applied Psychology, 68*(1), 43.

Bhagat, R. S., Allie, S. M., & Ford, D. L. (1995). Coping with stressful events: An empirical analysis. In R. Crandall & P. L. Perrewé (Eds.), *Occupational stress: A handbook.* Series in health psychology and behavioral medicine, 93–112. Philadelphia, PA: Taylor and Francis

Blair-Loy, M. (2003). *Competing devotions: Careers and family among women executives.* Cambridge, MA: Harvard University Press.

Blair-Loy, M., & Wharton, A. S. (2002). Employees' Use of Work-Family Policies and the Workplace Social Context. *Social Forces, 80*(3), 813-845.

Blau, F., Ferber, M. & Winkler, A. (1998). *The Economics of Women, Men, and Work (3rd ed.).* Upper Saddle River, NJ: Prentice-Hall.

Bloom, N. & Van Reenen, J. (2006). Management practices, work-life balance, and productivity: A review of some recent evidence. *Oxford Review of Economic Policy, 22* (4), 457-482.

Bond, F. & Bunce, D. (2001). Job control mediates change in a work reorganization intervention for stress reduction. *Journal of Occupational Health Psychology, 6* (4), 290-302.

Bray, D. W., Campbell, R. J., & Grant, D. L. (1974). *Formative years in business: A long-term AT&T study of managerial lives.* Wiley-Interscience.

Burke, R. J., Burgess, Z., & Oberrlaid, F. (2004). Do male psychologists benefit from organizational values supporting work-personal life balance?. *Equal Opportunities International, 23*(1/2), 97-107.

Butler, A., Grzywacz, J., Bass, B., & Linney, K. (2005). Extending the demands-control model: A daily diary study of job characteristics, work-family conflict and work-family facilitation. *Journal of occupational and organizational psychology, 78*(2), 155-169.

Caproni, P. J. (2004). Work/life balance: You can't get there from here. *The Journal of Applied Behavioral Science, 40*(2), 208-218.

Carlson, D.S., Kacmar, K.M. & Williams, L.J. (2000). Construction and initial validation of a multidimensional measure of work–family conflict. *Journal of Vocational Behavior, 56,* 249–76.

Carlson, D. S., Kacmar, K. M., Wayne, J.H. & Grzywacz, J. G. (2006). Measuring the positive side of the work-family interface: Development and validation of a work-family enrichment scale. *Journal of Vocational Behavior, 68*, 131–164.

Carlson, D. & Grzywacz, J. (2008). Reflections and future directions on measurement in work-family research. In K. Korabik, K. & D.Lero. (Eds.), *Handbook of Work and Family*, (pp.57-74). New York: Elsevier.

Chong, E. and Ma, X. (2010). The influence of individual factors, supervision and work environment on creative self-efficacy. *Creativity and Innovation Management, 19* (3), 233-247.

Chughtai, Aamir Ali. "Impact of job involvement on in-role job performance and organizational citizen-ship behaviour." Journal of Behavioral and Applied Management 9.2 (2008): 169.

Chung, P. J., Garfield, C. F., Elliott, M. N., Carey, C., Eriksson, C., & Schuster, M. A. (2007). Need for and use of family leave among parents of children with special health care needs. *American Academy of Pediatrics, 119*(5), e1047-e1055.

Cinamon, R. & Rich, Y. (2010). Work family relations: Antecedents and outcomes. *Journal of Career Assessment, 18*, 59-70.

Clark, S. C. (2000). Work/Family border theory: A new theory of work/family balance. *Human Relations, 53*(6), 747-770.

Clark, S. C. (2001). Work cultures and work/family balance. *Journal of Vocational Behavior,* *58*(3), 348-365. doi:10.1006/jvbe.2000.1759.

Colbeck, C. L., & Michael, P. W. (2006). The public scholarship: Reintegrating Boyer's our domain. *New Directions for Institutional Research, 114,* 43-52.

Colley, L. (2010). Central policies, local discretion: A review of employee access to worklife balance arrangements in a public sector agency. *Australian Bulletin ofLabour, 36(2),* 214-237

Crompton, R., Brockmann, M., & Lyonette, C. (2005). Attitudes, women's employment and the domestic division of labour a cross-national analysis in two waves. *Work, Employment & Society, 19*(2), 213-233.

Crooker K., Smith, F. L., and Tabak, F. (2002). Creating work-life balance: A model of pluralism across life domains. HRD Review. Vol.1, pp. 387-419.

De Cieri, H., Holmes, B., Abbot, J. & Pettit, T. (2005). Achievements and challenges for work/life balance strategies in Australian organizations. *International Journal of Human Resource Management, 16*(1): 90-103.

DeLong, T. & DeLong, C. (1992). Managers as Fathers: Hope on the homefront. *Human*

ignou   Work –Life Balance among Women Professionals

Resource Management, 31 (3), 171-181.

Den Dulk, L., & de Ruijster, J. (2008). Managing work-life policies: disruption versus dependency arguments. Explaining managerial attitudes towards employee utilization of work-life policies. *The International journal of human resources management*, 19(7), 1222-1293.

Den Dulk, L. Groeneveld, S. Ollier-Malaterre, A., & Valcour, M. (2012). National context in work-life research: A multi-level cross-national analysis of the adoption of work-life policies by employers in Europe, Paper presented at the Work and Family Researchers Network, New York, 14-16 June 2012.

Desai T, 2009, Work and Family in India, International Corner, 11(4), 1-2.

Desai T, Ishaya N, 2008 Predicting Work-Family Conflict via Perceived Involvement and Overload, Poster presented at American Psychological Association, Boston, MA, (August, 2008)

Desrochers, S., & Sargent, L. D. (2004). Boundary/border theory and work-family integration. *Organization Management Journal, 1*(1), 40-48.

Diefendorff, J. M., Brown, D. J., Kamin, A. M., & Lord, R. G. (2002). Examining the roles of job involvement and work centrality in predicting organizational citizenship behaviors and job performance. *Journal of Organizational Behavior, 23*(1), 93-108.

Drach-Zahavy, A., Somech, A. (2008). Coping with work-family conflict: integrating individual and organizational perspectives. In K. Korabik, Lcro, D.S., Whitehead, D.L. (Ed.), *Handbook of work-family integration* (pp. 267-286). Amsterdam: Elsevier.

Drago, R. & Williams, 1. (2000). A half-time tenure track proposal. *Change,* 6(6),46-51.

Drew, E. (2005). Work/life balance: Senior management champions or laggards? *Women in Management Review, 20* (4), 262-278.

Eby, L. T., Casper, W. J., Lockwood, A., Bordeaux, C., & Brinley, A. (2005). A retrospective on work and family research in IO/OB: A content analysis and review of the literature *Journal of Vocational Behavior, 66,* 124–197.

Edwards, J. & Rothbard, N. (2000). Mechanisms linking work and family: Clarifying the relationship between work and family constructs. *Academy of Management Review, 25,* 176-199.

Eisenberger, R., Stinglhamber, F., Vandenberghe, C., Sucharski, I. L., & Rhoades, L. (2002). Perceived supervisor support: contributions to perceived organizational support and employee retention. *Journal of applied psychology, 87*(3), 565.

Emslie, C., Hunt, K., & Macintyre, S. (2004). Gender, work-home, and morbidity amongst white-collar bank employees in the United Kingdom. *International Journal of Behavioral Medicine, 11*(3), 127-134.

Emslie, C. & Hunt, K (2009). 'Live to work' or 'work to live'? A qualitative study of gender and work-life balance among men and women in mid-life. *Gender, Work and Organization,* 16(1), 151-172.

English, H. (2003). *Gender on trial: Sexual stereotypes and work/life balance in the legal workplace.* New York: ALM.

European Commission. (2005). *Reconciliation of work and private life: A comparative review of thirty European countries.* Luxembourg: Office for Official Publications of the European Communities.

Eurostat. (2006). EU Labour Force Survey, Principal Results 2005.

European Working Conditions Observatory. (2008). "Equality policies and practices in companies."

European Working Conditions Observatory. (2009). Working time in European Union: Spain, 2009.

Evans, J. M. (2002). Work/family reconciliation, gender wage equity and occupational segregation: The role of firms and public policy. *Canadian Public Policy, 18*(Suppl.), 187-216.

Falkenberg, L., & Monachello, M. (1990). Dual-career and dual-income families: Do they have different needs?. *Journal of business ethics, 9*(4-5), 339-351

Finegold, D., Mohrman, S., & Spreitzer, G. M. (2002). Age effects on the predictors of technical workers' commitment and willingness to turnover. *Journal of Organizational Behavior, 23*(5), 655-674

Finkel, S. K & Olswang, S. G. (1996). Child rearing as a career impediment to women assistant professors. The Review ofHigher Education, 19(2), 123-139.

Finkel, S. K, Olswang, S., & She, N. (1994). Childbirth, tenure, and promotion for women faculty. The Review of Higher Education, 17(3),259-270.

Fisher,K.and Layte, R. (2002): Measuring Work-Life Balance Using Time Diary Data. *electronic international journal of time use research.* 2-13.

Friedman, S. D. & Greenhaus, 1. H. (2000). *Work and family--allies or enemies? What happenswhen business professionals confront life choices.* Oxford, England: Oxford University Press.

Frone, Michael R., Marcia Russell, and M. Lynne Cooper. "Antecedents and outcomes of work-family conflict: testing a model of the work-family inter-face." Journal of applied psychology 77.1 (1992): 65

Frone, M. R. (2003). Work-family balance. In J. C. Quick & L. E. Tetrick (eds), *Handbook of Occupational Health Psychology* (pp. 143–162). Washington, DC: American Psychological Association.

Frone, M. R., & Yardley, J. K. (1996). Workplace family-supportive programmes: Predictors of employed parents' importance ratings. Journal of Occupational and Organizational Psychology, 69, 351-366.

Frone, M. R., Yardley, J. K., & Markel, K. S. (1997). Developing and testing an integrative model of the work-family interface. Journal of Vocational Behavior, 50, 145–167.

Galinsky, E., & Johnson, A. A. (1998). *Reframing the business case for work-life initiatives.* Families & Work Inst.

Gappa, 1. M., Austin, A. E., & Trice, A. G. (2007). *Rethinkingfaculty work: Higher education's strategic imperative.* San Francisco, CA: Jossey-Bass.

Garey, A. I. (1999). Motherhood on the night shift. In *Weaving Work and Motherhood* (pp. 108–139). Philadelphia: Temple University Press.

Giele, J. Z., & Elder, G. H. (Eds.). (1998). *Methods of life course research: Qualitative and quantitative approaches*. Sage Publications.

Gilbreath, B. & Benson, P. (2004). The contribution of supervisor behaviour to employee psychological well-being. *Work & Stress, 18* (3), 255-266.

Gliem, R. R., & Gliem, J. A. (2003). Calculating, interpreting, and reporting Cronbach's alpha reliability coefficient for Likert-type scales. Midwest Research-to-Practice Conference in Adult, Continuing, and Community Education

Glubczynski, J., Kossek, E. E. and Lambert, S. J. (2003), A question of leadership: What can managers do to promote work-life balance for themselves and others? *Leadership in Action*, 23: 12–13.

Godbey, G., Crawford, D. & Shen, X. (2010). Assessing hierarchical leisure constraints theory after two decades. *Journal of Leisure Research, 42*, 111-134.

Goh, Zen, Remus Ilies, and Kelly Schwind Wilson. "Supportive supervisors improve employees' daily lives: The role supervisors play in the impact of dai-ly workload on life satisfaction via work–family conflict." Journal of Vocational Behavior 89 (2015): 65-73.

Grant, L., Kennelly, 1., & Ward, K. B. (2000). Revisiting the gender, marriage, and parenthood puzzle in scientific careers. *Women's Studies Quarterly, 28*(112),62-85.

Greenblatt, E. (2002). Work/life balance: Wisdom or whining. *Organizational Dynamics, 31*(2), 177-193.

Greenhaus, J. H. & Beutell, N. J. (1985). Sources ofconflict between work and family roles. *Academy of Management Review, 10(*1), 76-88.

Greenhaus, J., Collins, K. & Shaw, J. (2003). The relation between work-family balance and quality of life. *Journal of Vocational Behavior, 63*, 510-531.

Greenhaus, J. H., Collins, K. M., Singh, R., & Parasuraman, S. (1997). Work and family influences on departure from public accounting. *Journal of Vocational Behavior, 50*(2), 249-270

Greenhaus, J. H., & Kopelman, R. E. (1981). Conflict between work and nonwork roles: Implications for the career planning process. *Human Resource Planning, 4*(1), 1-10.

Greenhaus, J. H. & Powell, G. N. (2006). When work and family are allies: A theory of work- family enrichment. *Academy of Management Review, 31* (1), 72-92.

Grzywacz, J. G. & Marks, N. F. (2000). Reconceptualizing the work-family interface: An

ignou   Work –Life Balance among Women Professionals

ecological perspective on the correlates of positive and negative spillover between work and family. Journal of Occupational Health Psychology, 1, 111–126.

Grzywacz, J. G. & Butler, A.B. (2005). The impact of job characteristics on work-to-family facilitation: Testing a theory and distinguishing a construct. *Journal of Occupational Health Psychology, 10,* 97–109.

Grzywacz, J.G. & Carlson, D.S. (2007). Conceptualizing work–family balance: Implications for practice and research. *Advances in Developing Human Resources, 9,* 455–71

Guendouzi, J. (2006). "The guilt thing:" Balancing domestic and professional roles. *Journal of Marriage and Family, 68*(4), 901-909.

Guest, D. E. (1998). Is the psychological contract worth taking seriously?. *Journal of organizational behavior,* 649-664.

Guest, D. E. (2002). Perspectives on the study of work-life balance. *Social Science Information, 41*(2), 255-279.

Gutek, B. A., Searle, S., & Klepa, L. (1991). Rational versus gender role explanations for work-family conflict. *Journal of applied psychology, 76*(4), 560.

Haar, J. & Roche, M. (2010). Family supportive organization perceptions and employee outcomes: The mediating effects of life satisfaction. *The International Journal of Human Resources Management, 21* (7), 999-1014.

Hall, D. T. (1972). A model of coping with role conflict: The role behavior of college educated women. *Administrative Science Quarterly, 17,* 471–486.

Hall, D. & Richter, J. (1988). Balancing work life and home life: What can organizations do to help? *The Academy of Management Executive, 2* (3), 213-223.

Haworth, J. & Lewis, S. (2005). Work, leisure and well-being. *British Journal of Guidance & Counselling, 33,* 67-79.

Harrington, B., Van Deusen, F., Ladge, 1. (2010). *The new dad: Exploring fatherhood within a career context.* Newton, MA: Boston College Center for Work & Family.

Harrington, B. & Ladge, 1. J. (2009). Got talent? It isn't hard to find. *The Shriver report: A woman's nation changes everything.*

Hayman, J. (2005). Psychometric Assessment of an Instrument Designed to Measure Work Life Balance, *Research and Practice in Human Resource Management,* 13(1), 85-91.

Hertz, Rosanna. (1986). *More equal than others: Women and men in dual-career marriages.* Berkeley: California Press.

ignou   Work –Life Balance among Women Professionals

Hewlett, S. A. (2007). *Off-ramps and on-ramps: Keeping talented women on the road to success.* Boston, MA: Harvard Business School Press.

Higgins, C., Duxbury, L., & Lee, C. (1994). Impact of life-cycle stage and gender on the ability to balance work and family responsibilities. *Family Relations, 43*(2), 144-150.

Higgins, C., Duxbury, L. & Lyons, S. (2010). Coping with overload and stress: Men and women in dual-earner families. *Journal of Marriage and Family, 72*, 847-859.

Hill, E. J. (2005). Work-family facilitation and conflict, working fathers and mothers, work family stressors and support. *Journal of Family Issues, 26*(6), 793-819.

Hill, S., Bahniuk, M., Dobos, J. & Rouner, D. (2001). Mentoring and other communication support in the academic setting. *Group and Organization Management, 14,* 355-68.

Hill, E. J., Martinson, V., & Ferris, M. (2004). New-concept part-time employment as a work-family adaptive strategy for women professionals with small children. *Family Relations, 53*(3), 282-292.

Howard, A., & Bray, D. W. (1988). *Managerial lives in transition: Advancing age and changing times.* Guilford Press.

House, J. S. (1981). *Work stress and social support*. Addison-Wesley Pub. Co

Hyman, J., & Summers, J. (2004). Lacking balance? Work-life employment practices in the modern economy. *Personnel Review, 33*(4), 418-429.

Hyman, J., Baldry, C., Scholarios, D., & Bunzel, D. (2003). Work–life imbalance in call centres and software development. *British Journal of Industrial Relations, 41*(2), 215-239.

Innstrand, S. T., Langballe, E. M., & Falkum, E. (2010). Exploring occupational differences in work–family interaction: who is at risk?. *International Journal of Stress Management, 17*(1), 38.

Ironson, G. (1992). Work, job stress, and health. In S. Zedeck (Ed). *Work families, and organizations* (pp. 33-69). San Francisco, CA: Jossey-Bass, Inc.

Jennings, J. & McDougald, M. (2007). Work-family interface experiences and coping strategies: Implications for entrepreneurship research and practice. *Academy of Management Review, 32* (3), 747-760.

Jex, S & Guadonowski, D. (1992). Efficacy beliefs and work stress: An exploratory study. *Journal of Organizational Behaviour, 13*, 509-517.

Johnsrud, L. K., Heck, R. H., & Rosser, V. J. (2000, January/February). Morale matters: Midlevel administrators and their intent to leave. *Journal of Higher Education, 71*, 34-59.

Johnsrud, L. K., & Heck, R. H. (1994). A university' s faculty: Explaining those who leave and those who stay. Journal of Higher Education Management, 10, (1): 71-84.

Johnsrud, L. K. (2002). Measuring the quality of faculty and administrative worklife: Implications for college and university campuses. Research in Higher Education, 43(3), 379-395.

Johnsrud, L. K., & Rosser, V. J. (2002). Faculty members' morale and their intention to leave. Journal of Higher Education, 73(4), 518-541.

Judge, T. & Colquitt, J. (2004). Organizational justice and stress: The mediating role of work- family conflict. *Journal of Applied Psychology, 89* (3), 395-404.

Judiesch, M. K., & Lyness, K. S. (1999). Left behind? The impact of leaves of absence on managers' career success. *Academy of management journal, 42*(6), 641-651.

Kalliath, T. & Brough, P. (2008). Work-life balance: A review ofthe meaning ofthe balance construct. *Journal ofManagement and Organization* 14, 323-327.

Kanugo, R. N (1982a). Measurement of job and work involvement. Journal of Applied Psychology, 67 (3). 341-349.

ignou   Work –Life Balance among Women Professionals

Kanungo, R. N. (1982b). Work alienation: An integrative approach. New York: Praeger

King, Lynda A., et al. "Family support inventory for workers: A new measure of perceived social support from family members." Journal of Organizational Behavior 16.3 (1995): 235-258.

Kapoor, J., Bhardwaj, G., & Pestonjee, D. M. (1999). Enquiry into the various facets of women's careers. IIM Ahmedabad.

Keene, J. R., & Quadagno, J. (2004). Predictors of perceived work-family balance: Gender difference or gender similarity? Sociological Perspectives, 47(1), 1-23.

Kelly, E. L., Kossek, E. E., Hammer, L. B., Durham, M., Bray, J., Chermack, K., Murphy, L.A., & Kaskubar, D. (2008). Chapter 7: Getting there from here: research on the effects of work-family initiatives on work-family conflict and business outcomes. The Academy of Management Annals, 2 (1), 305 – 349.

Khan, F., Yusoff, R. M., & Khan, A. (2014). Job demands, burnout and resources in teaching a conceptual review. World Applied Sciences Journal, 30(1), 20-28.

Kirchmeyer, C. (1992). Perceptions of nonwork-to-work spillover: Challenging the common view of conflictridden domain relationships. Basic and Applied Social Psychology, 13, 231–249

Kirchmeyer, C. (1993). Nonwork-to-work spillover: A more balanced view of the experiences and coping of professional women and men. *Sex Roles, 28*, 531–552.

Kirshmeyer, C. (1995). Managing the work-nonwork boundary: an assessment of organizational responses. Human Relations, 48 (5), 515-536.

Kirchmeyer, C. (2000). Work–life initiatives: Greed or benevolence regarding workers' time. In C.L. Cooper & D.M. Rousseau (Eds.). *Trends in Organisational Behavior*, 7, 79–93. Chichester: John Wiley & Sons.

Kofodimos, J.R. (1995). Beyond Work-Family Programs: confronting and Resolving the Underlying Causes of Work-Personal Life Conflict. Greensboro, NC: Center for Creative Leadership.

Komarraju, M. (1997). The work-family interface in India. *Integrating work and family: Challenges for a changing world, Westport, CT: Quorum Books*, 104-114.

Kossek, E. E. & Friede, A. (2006). The business case: managerial perspectives on Work and Family. In M. Pitt-Catsouphes, E.E. Kossek, & S.Sweet (Eds), *The Work and Family Handbook. Multi-Disciplinary Perspectives and Approaches*. Mahwah, NJ: Lawrence Erlbaum Associates.

Kossek, E. E., Noe, R. A., & DeMarr, B. J. (1999). Work-family role synthesis: individual and organizational determinants. *International Journal of Conflict Management, 10*(2), 102-129.

Kossek, E. E. & Hammer, L.B. (2008). Supervisor work/life training gets results. Harvard Business Review, November, 1-3.

Kossek, E. E., Noe, R. A., & DeMarr, B. J. (1999). Work-family role synthesis: individual and organizational determinants. International Journal of Conflict Management, 10(2), 102-129.

Kossek, E.E., Lewis, S., & Hammer, L. B. (2010). Work-life initiatives and organizational change: Overcoming mixed messages to move from the margin to the mainstream. Human Relations, 63(1), 3-19.

Kossek, E., & Ozeki, C. (1998). Work–family conflict, policies, and the job–life satisfaction relationship: A review and directions for organizational behavior–human resources research. *Journal of applied psychology, 83*(2), 139.

Kossek E.E, Ozeki C. (1999). Bridging the work-family policy and productivity gap: A literature review. Community, Work & Family, 2, 7-32.

Lambert, S. J., & Haley-Lock, A. (2004). The organizational stratification of opportunities for work-life balance. *Community, Work & Family, 7*(2), 179-195.

Lambert, S.J. (2000). Added benefits: The link between work-life benefits and Organizational citizenship behavior. Academy of Management Journal, 43, 801-15.

Lambert, A. D., Marler, J. H., & Gueutal, H. G. (2008). Individual differences: Factors affecting employee utilization of flexible work arrangements. Journal of Vocational Behavior, 73(1), 107-117

Languilaire, J.C. (2007). Segmentation and integration of work and personal life: how do French middle-mangers make choices? *Paper presented at the International Conference of Work and Family, 2007.*

Languilaire, J-C. (2009). Experiencing work/non-work. *Theorising individuals' process of integrating and segmenting work, family, social and private.* Jönköping International Business School.

Lapierre, L. M., & Allen, T. D. (2006). Work-supportive family, family- supportive supervision, use of organizational benefits, and problem-focused coping: Implications for work–family conflict and employee well-being. *Journal of Occupational Health Psychology, 11,* 169–181.

Lazarus, R. S., & Folkman, S. (1984). Stress, appraisal, and coping. New York: Springer.

Lee, J. A. & Phillips, S. 1. (2006). Work and family: Can you have it all? *The Psychologist*

Manager Journal, 9(1), 41-57.

Lewis, S. (1997) Family Friendly' Employment Policies: A Route to Changing
Organizational Culture or Playing About at the Margins? Gender, Work and Organization, 4,
(1), 13-23.

Lewis, S. (2001). Restructuring workplace cultures: the ultimate work-family challenge?
Women in Management Review, 16: 21-29.

Lewis, S., & Dyer, J. (2002). Towards a culture for work-life integration?. *The New World of
Work. Challenges and Opportunities, Malden, MA, Blackwell Publishers,* 302-316.

Lewis, S. (2003). The integration of paid work and the rest of life. Is post- industrial work the
new leisure? Leisure Studies, 22 (4), 343-355.

Lewis, S., Cooper, C. (2005). Work-Life Integration. Case Studies of Organization Change.
London, John Wiley & Sons.

Lewis, S., Gambles, R., & Rapoport R. (2007). The Constraints of a „Work-Life Balance
Approach: An International Perspective. *International Journal of Human Resource
Management,* 18 (3), 360-37.

Lewis, J. & Giullari, S. (2005). The adult worker model family, gender equality and care: the

ignou   Work –Life Balance among Women Professionals

search for new policy principles and the possibilities and problems of a capability approach. Economy and Society, 34 (1): 76-104.

Lewis, S. & Rajan-Rankin, S. (2012). Deconstructing 'Family supportive cultures: A vision for the future. In: S. Poelmans, J. Greenhaus, & M. las Heras, New Frontiers in Work-Family Research: A Vision for the Future in a Global World. Palgrave Marcmillan.

Lewis S, & Smithson, J. (2001) Sense of entitlement to support for the reconciliation of employment and family life. Human Relations, 55, 1455- 81.

Lewis, S. & Taylor, K. (1996) Evaluating the impact of family-friendly employment policies: a case study. In S. Lewis and J. Lewis (eds.) The Work-Family Challenge. Rethinking Employment. London: Sage.

Lirio, P., Lee, M. D., Williams, M. L., Haugen, L. K., & Kossek, E. E. (2008). The inclusion challenge with reduced-load professionals: The role of the manager. *Human Resource Management, 47*(3), 443-461.

Loerch, K. J., Russell, J. E., & Rush, M. C. (1989). The relationships among family domain variables and work-family conflict for men and women. *Journal of Vocational Behavior, 35*(3), 288-308.

Lowe, G. S., Krahn, H., & Tanner, J. (1988). Young people's explanations of unemployment. *Youth and Society, 19*(3), 227.

Macdonald, M., Phipps, S., & Lynne, L. (2005). Taking its toll: The influence of paid and unpaid work on women's well-being. *Feminist Economics, 11*(1), 63-94.

MacEwen, K. E., & Barling, J. (1994). Daily consequences of work interference with family and family interference with work. *Work & Stress, 8*(3), 244-254.

MacInnes, J. (2005). Work-life balance and the demand for reduction in working hours: Evidence from the British social attitudes survey 2002. *British Journal of Industrial Relations, 43*, 273-295.

Mauno,S. and Kinnunen, U. (1999) "The effects of job stressors on marital satisfaction in Finnish dual earner couples". *Journal of organizational behavior.* 20(6): 879-95.

Marks, S.R. & MacDermid, S.M. (1996). Multiple roles and the self: a theory of role balance. *Journal of Marriage and the Family*, 58 (2), 417-432.

Marks, S. R. (1977). Multiple roles and role strain: Some notes on human energy, time, and commitment. American Sociological Review, 42, 921– 936

Marshall K, (2006). Converging gender roles. *Statistics Canada,*1-13.

ignou   Work –Life Balance among Women Professionals

Martins, L., Eddleston, K. & Veiga, J. (2002). Moderators of the relationship between work family conflict and career satisfaction. *Academy of Management Journal,45* (2), 399-409.

Martin, B., León, C., Masuda, A. D., & Chinchilla, N. (2010). Work-life balance in Europe: A shared concern. In N. Chinchilla, M. Las Heras, & A. Masuda, (Eds.), Balancing Work and Family: A Practical Guide to Help Organizations Meet the Global Workforce Challenge. Amrest: HRD Press, 79-98

Mason, M. A. & Ekman, E. M. (2007). Mothers on the fast track: How a new generation can balance family and careers. New York: Oxford University Press.

Mason, M. A. & Goulden, M. (2004). Marriage and baby blues: Redefining gender equity in the academy. The ANNALS of the American Academy of Political and Social Science, 596, 86-103.

Mason, M. A.(2009). Is tenure a trap? Not if the tenure system is adapted to suit the modern realities of professors' lives. Chronicle of Higher Education

Mathew, R. V., & Panchanatham, N. (2011). An exploratory study on the work-life balance of women entrepreneurs in South India. *Asian academy of management journal, 16*(2), 77-105.

Matos, K. & Galinsky, E. (2011). *Workplace flexibility in the United States: A status report.*

New York, NY: Families and Work Institute and Society for Human Resources
Management

Maxwell, G. & McDougall, M. (2004). Work-life balance. *Public Management Review, 6* (3),
377-393.

Maxwell, G. (2005). Checks and balances: The role of managers in work-life balance policies
and practices. *Journal of Retailing and Consumer Services, 12,* 179-189.

McCubbin, M. A. (1993). Family stress theory and the development of nursing knowledge
about family adaptation. In S.L. Feetham, S.B. Meister, J. M. Bell, & C. L. Gills (Eds.), The
nursing family. New Bury Park: Sage Publications, 46-58.

McCubbin, M. A., & McCubbin, H. I. (1991). Family stress theory and assessment: The
resiliency model of family stress, adjustment, and adaptation. In H. I. McCubbin & A. I.
Thompson (Eds.), Family assessment inventories fro research and practice (pp. 3-32).
Madison: University of Wisconsin-Madison.

McCubbin, H. I., & McCubbin, M. A. (1993). Families coping with illness: The resiliency
model of family stress, adjustment, and adaptation. In C. B. Danielson, B. Hamel-Bissell, &
P. Winstead-Fry (Eds.), Families, health, and illness. St. Louis, MI: Allison Miller.

McCubbin, L. I., & McCubbin, M.A., Patterson, J. M., Cauble, A. E., Wilson, L. R., and
ignou   Work –Life Balance among Women Professionals

Warwick, W. (1983). CHIP-Coping health inventory for parents: An assessment of parental coping patterns in the care of the chronically ill child. Journal of Marriage and Family, 45(2), 359-370.

McCubbin, H., McCubbin, M., Thompson, A., & Thompson, E. (1995). Resiliency in ethnic families: A conceptual model for predicting family adjustment and adaptation. In H. McCubbin, M. McCubbin, A. Thompson, & J. Fromer (Eds.), Resiliency in ethnic minority families (Vol. 1, pp. 3-48). Madison, WI: Univeristy of Wisconsin Press.

McCubbin, H., & Patterson, J. (1983). The family stress process: The double ABCX model of family adjustment and adaptation. Marriage and Family Review, 6(1-2), 7-37.

Md-Sidin, S., Sambasivan, M. & Ismail, I. (2008) Relationship between work-family conflict and quality of life. Journal of Management Psychology, 25, 58-81.

Medved, C. E. (2004). The everyday accomplishment of work and family: Exploring practical actions in daily routines. Communication Studies, 55 (1), 128-145.

Mennino, S. F., Rubin, B. A., & Brayfield, A. (2005). Home-to-job and job-to-home spillover: The impact of company policies and workplace culture, The Sociological Quarterly, 46(1), 107-135.

Milkie, M. A., & Peltola, P. (1999). Playing all the roles: Gender and the work-family balancing act. *Journal of Marriage and the Family, 61*(2), 476-490.

Moreno, L. (2004). Spain's transition to New Risks: a farewell to 'superwomen''. En Taylor-Gooby, P. (Ed.), *New Risks, New Welfare: The Transformation of the European Welfare*. Oxford: Oxford University Press, 137-160.

Naldini, M. (2003) *The Family in the Mediterranean Welfare States*. Londres: Frank Cass.

Nippert-Eng, C. E. (1996). *Home and Work : Negotiating Boundaries trough Everyday Life*. Chicago & London: The University Chicago Press.

Narayan, A., & Bhardwaj, G. (2005). Dual career nuclear families in India: Attitudes and social support. *Indian Journal of Industrial Relations*, 79-93.

Ng, T. W., Eby, L. T., Sorensen, K. L., & Feldman, D. C. (2005). Predictors of objective and subjective career success: A meta-analysis. *Personnel psychology, 58*(2), 367-408.

Ng, Thomas WH. "The incremental validity of or-ganizational commitment, organizational trust, and organizational identification." Journal of Vocational Behavior 88 (2015): 154-163.

Nunnally, J. (1978). Psychometric methods.

OECD (2007). *Reconciling Work and Family Life – A Synthesis of Findings for OECD countries*, 29, November 2007.

Pal, S., & Saksvik, P. Ø. (2008). Work-family conflict and psychosocial work environment stressors as predictors of job stress in a cross-cultural study. *International Journal of Stress Management, 15*(1), 22.

Parasuraman, S et al. "Work and family varia-bles, entrepreneurial career success, and psychologi-cal well-being." Journal of Vocational Behavior 48.3 (1996): 275-300.

Parasuraman, S., & Greenhaus, J. H. (1997). The changing world of work and family. In S. Parasuraman, & J. H. Greenhaus (Eds.), *Integrating Work and Family: Challenges and Choices for a Changing World*. Westport, CN: Quorum Books.

Paruthi, M., & Phardwaj, G. (1985). Family Environment and Job-Related Tension across Five Levels in a Food Processing Industry. *Indian Journal of Industrial Relations, 20*(3), 310-318

Philipsen, Maike, I. (2008). *Challenges of the faculty career for women*. San Francisco: Jossey-Bass.

Pickering, D. I. (2006). *The relationship between work-life conflict/work-life balance and operational effectiveness in the Canadian Forces* (No. DRDC-TR-2006-243). DEFENCE RESEARCH AND DEVELOPMENT TORONTO (CANADA)

ignou   Work –Life Balance among Women Professionals

Pleck, J. H. (1985). Working wives/working husbands.

Pocock, B. (2005). Work-life 'balance'in Australia: Limited progress, dim prospects. *Asia Pacific Journal of Human Resources*, *43*(2), 198-209.

Poelmans, S. (2003). Editorial. The multi-level "fit" model of work and family (Editorial introduction to special issue on "Theoretical frameworks for cross-cultural research on work and family". International Journal of Cross-Cultural Management, 3(3), 267-274.

Poelmans, S., Kalliath, T., & Brough, P. (2008). Achieving Work-Life Balance: Current theoretical and practice issues. Journal of Management & Organization, 14 (3), 227-238

Poelmans, S., Chinchilla, N. & Cardona, P.(2003). Family-friendly HRM Policies and the Employment Relationship, International Journal of Manpower, 24(3): 128-47.

Poelmans, S., & Sahibzada, K. (2004). A multi-level model for studying the context and impact work–family policies and culture in organizations. Human Resource Management Review, 14, 409-431.

Poelmans, S. & Beham, B. (2008). The moment of truth: Conceptualizing managerial work life policy allowance decisions. *Journal of Occupational and Organizational Psychology*, *81*, 3, 393-410

ignou   Work –Life Balance among Women Professionals

Poelmans, S., Stepanova, O. & Masuda, A. (2008). Spillover between personal and professional life: Definitions, antecedents, consequences, and strategies. In K. Korabik, K. & D.Lero. (Eds.), Handbook of Work and Family. New York: Elsevier.

Porter, S. & Ayman, R. (2010). Work flexibility as a mediator of the relationship between work- family conflict and intention to quit. *Journal of Management & Organization, 16*, 411-424.

Potgieter, S. & Barnard, A. (2010). The construction of work-life balance: The experience of black employees in a call-centre environment. *SA Journal of Industrial Psychology, 31*, 892-900.

Purcell, J., & Hutchinson, S. (2007). Front-line managers as agents in the HRM-performance causal chain: theory, analysis and evidence. *Human Resource management journal, 17*(1), 3-20.

Rajadhyaksha, U., & Smita, S. (2004). Tracing a timeline for work and family research in India. *Economic and Political Weekly*, 1674-1680.

Rapoport, R., Bailyn, L., Fletcher, J., & Pruitt, B. (2002). Beyond Work-Family Balance. *Advancing Gender Equity and Workplace Performance*. San Francisco: Jossey-Bass.

Rau, B.L., & Hyland, M.A.M. (2002). Role conflict and Flexible work arrangements: the

ignou   Work –Life Balance among Women Professionals

effects on applicant attraction. *Personnel Psychology, 55* (1), 111-136

Reddy, N. K., Vranda, M. N., Ahmed, A., Nirmala, B. P., & Siddaramu, B. (2010). Work–Life Balance among Married Women Employees. *Indian journal of psychological medicine, 32*(2), 112.

Rehman, S., & Azam Roomi, M. (2012). Gender and work-life balance: a phenomenological study of women entrepreneurs in Pakistan. *Journal of Small Business and Enterprise Development, 19*(2), 209-228.

Reynolds, L. E. (2005). Surrendering the dream: Early career conflict and faculty dissatisfaction thresholds. *Journal of Career Development, 32,* 107-121.

Robbins, Stephen P., and Tim Judge. Essentials of organizational behavior. Pearson Higher Ed, 2013.

Roehling, P. V., Roehling, M. V., & Moen, P. (2001). The relationship between work-life policies and practices and employee loyalty: A life course perspective. *Journal of Family and Economic Issues, 22*(2), 141-170.

Rosenfield, S. (1989). The effects of women's employment: Personal control and sex differences in mental health. *Journal of Health and Social Behavior, 30*(1), 77-91.

ignou   Work –Life Balance among Women Professionals

Rothbard, N. (2001). Enriching or depleting? The dynamics of engagement in work and family roles. *Administrative Science Quarterly, 46*, 655-684.

Rotondo, D. M., Carlson, D. S., & Kincaid, J. F. (2003). Coping with multiple dimensions of work–family conflict. *Personnel Review, 32*, 275–296.

Rout, U. R., Lewis, S., & Kagan, C. (1999). Work and family roles: Indian career women in India and the West. *Indian Journal of Gender Studies, 6*(1), 91-103

Ruderman, M., Ohlott, P., Panzer, K. & King, S. (2002). Benefits of multiple roles for managerial women. *Academy of Management Journal, 45* (2), 369-386.

Sallee, M. W. (2008). Work and family balance: How community college faculty cope. New Directionsfor Community Colleges, 142,81-91.

Sallee, M. W. (2012). The ideal worker or the ideal father: Organizational structures and culture in the gendered university. Research in Higher Education, 53(7), 782-802.

Sandhu, H. S., & Mehta, R. (2006). Work-family conflict among women executives in service sector: an empirical study. *Journal of Advances in Management Research, 3*(2), 68-80.

Sarkar, S. (2011). *International Journal of Strategic Organization and Behavioural Science: Vol. 1, No. 1.* Universal-Publishers.

Schaufeli, W. B., & Bakker, A. B. (2004). Job demands, job resources, and their relationship with burnout and engagement: A multi-sample study. *Journal of organizational Behavior, 25*(3), 293-315.

Seo, Jae Young. "Job involvement of part-time fac-ulty: exploring associations with distributive justice, underemployment, work status congruence, and em-powerment." University of Iowa (2013).

Sheldon, K., & Niemiec, C. (2006). It's not just the amount that counts: Balanced need satisfaction also affects well-being. *Journal of Personality and Social Psychology,* 91, 331-341

Secret, M., & Sprang, G. (2001). The effect of family-friendly workplace environment on work-family stress of employed parents. *Journal of Social Service Research, 28*(2), 21-45.

Seron, C. & Ferris, K. (1995). Negotiating professionalism: The gendered social capital of flexible time. *Work and Occupation, 22,* 22-47.

Sharma, S. (1999). Multiple-roles and women's health: A multi-linear model. *Equal Opportunities International, 18*(8), 16-23.

Smithson, J., & Stokoe, E. H. (2005). Discourses of work-life balance: Negotiating 'genderblind' terms in organizations. *Gender, Work and Organization, 12*(2), 147-168.

Sorcinelli, M. D., & Near, J. P. (1989). Relations between work and life away from work among university faculty. The Journal ofHigher Education, 60(1), 59-81.

Spector, P. E. (1987). Method variance as an artifact in self-reported affect and perceptions at work: Myth or significant problem?. *Journal of Applied Psychology, 72*(3), 438.

Spencer-Dawe. E. (2005). Lone mothers in employment: Seeking rational solutions to role strain. *Journal of Social Welfare and Family Law, 27*, 251-264.

Suchet, M., & Barling, J. (1986). Employed mothers: Interrole conflict, spouse support and marital functioning. *Journal of Organizational Behavior, 7*(3), 167-178.

Stephens, G. K., & Sommer, S. M. (1993). Work-family conflict, job attitudes, and workplace social support: Investigations of measurement and moderation. In *meeting of Academy of Management, Atlanta, Georgia*

Stephen, L. (1994). *Hear my testimony: María Teresa Tula, human rights activist of El Salvador.* Boston: South End Press.

Taştan, Seçil Bal. "The influences of participative organizational climate and self-leadership on inno-vative behavior and the roles of job involvement and proactive personality: A Survey in the Context of SMEs in Izmir." Procedia-Social and Behavioral Sciences 75 (2013): 407-419.

Tausig, M. & Fenwick, R. (2001). Unbinding time: Alternate work schedules and work-life balance. *Journal of Family and Economic Issues, 22*(2), 101-120.

Thriveni, K. (2011). Impact Of Stress On Work-Life-Balance Of Women Employees With Reference To BPO and Education Sectors In Bangalore. *International Journal Of Research In Commerce, It & Management, 1*(7).

Thomas, L. & Ganster, D. C. (1995). Impact of family-supportive work variables on work family conflict and strain: A control perspective. *Journal of Applied Psychology, 80,* 6-15.

Thompson, C. A., Thomas, C. C., & Maier, M. (1992). Work–family conflict and the bottom line: Reassessing corporate policies and initiatives. In U. Sekaran & F. T. Leong (Eds.), Womanpower: Managing in times of demographic turbulence (pp. 59–84). Newbury Park, CA: Sage

Thompson, C. A., Beauvais, L. L. & Lyness, K. S. (1999). When work–family benefits are not enough: The influence of work–family culture on benefit utilization, organizational attachment, and work–family conflict. *Journal of Vocational Behavior, 54,* 392–415.

ignou   Work –Life Balance among Women Professionals

Thompson, C. A., Jahn, Eileen W., Kopelman, Richard E., Prottas, David J. (2004).

Perceived organizaitonal family support: a longitudinal and multilevel analysis. *Journal of Managerial Issues, 16*(4), 545-565.

Thompson, C.A., Poelmans, S.A.Y., Allen, T.D. & Andreassi, J.K. (2007). On the importance of coping: A model and new directions for research on work and family. In P.L. Perrewé & D.C. Ganster, *Exploring the Work and Non-work Interface, Research in Occupational Stress and Well Being* (pp. 73-113), *volume 6.* Elsevier Ltd.

Thompson, C. A. (2008). Barriers to the implementation and usage ofwork-life policies. In S. A. Y. Poelmans & P. Caligiuri (Eds). *Harmonizing work, family, andpersonal life: From policy to practice* (pp. 209-234). Cambridge, England: Cambridge University Press.

Tobia, C. (2001). Working and mothering. Women's strategies in Spain, *EuropeanSocieties, 3* (3): 339-371.

Ulshafer, S., Potgeisser, M. & Lima, T. (2005). Concierge services help deliver better work/life balance at Bronson Healthcare Group. *Journal of Organizational Excellence, 24* (3), 23- 30.

Ungerson, C., & Yeandle, S. (2005). Care workers and work-life balance: the example of domiciliary careworkers. D. M. Hounston. (ed.), *Work-life balance in the 21st century.* Hampshire: Palgrave Macmillan.

Van Daalen, G., Willemsen, T. M., & Sanders, K. (2006). Reducing work–family conflict through different sources of social support. *Journal of Vocational Behavior, 69*(3), 462-476.

Van den Broeck, A., Vansteenkiste, M. & Has De Witte, W. (2010). Unemployed individuals work values and job flexibility: An explanation from expectancy-value theory and self determination theory. *Applied Psychology: An International Review, 59* (2), 296-317.

Veenhoven, R. (1991). Is happiness relative? *Social Indicators Research,* 235-247.

Voydanoff, P. (2002). Linkages between the workfamily interface and work, family, and individual outcomes. Journal of Family Issues, 23, 138–164.

Voydanoff, P (2008). Work Role Characteristics, Family Structure Demands, and Work/Family Conflict. *Journal of Marriage and Family,* 50 (3), 749-761

Watkins, K. (1995). Changing managers" defensive reasoning about work/family conflict. *Journal of Management, 14* (2) 77-88.

Wang, P., Lawler, J. & Shi, K. (2010). Work-family conflict, self-efficacy, job satisfaction, and gender: Evidences from Asia. *Journal of Leadership & Organizational Studies, 17* (3), 298-308.

ignou   Work –Life Balance among Women Professionals

Ward, K. A. & Wolf-Wendel, L. (2004a). Academic motherhood: Managing complex roles in research universities. *The Review of Higher Education,* 27(2),233-257.

Ward, K. & Wolf-Wendel, L. (2004b). Fear factor: How safe is it to make time for family? *Academy, 90(6).*

Ward, K. & Wolf-Wendel, L. E. (2005). Work and family perspectives from research university faculty. In J. W. Curtis (Ed.), *The challenge of balancing faculty careers and family work* (pp. 41-65). San Francisco, CA: Jossey-Bass.

Warren, T. (2004). Working part-time: Achieving a successful work-life balance? *The British Journal of Sociology, 55,* 99-122.

Wayne, J. H., Musisca, N. & Fleeson, W. (2004). Considering the role of personality in the work-family experience: Relationships of the big five to work-family conflict and facilitation. *Journal of Vocational Behavior, 64,* 108–130.

Wesley, J. R., & Muthuswamy, P. R. (2005). Work-family conflict in India-An empirical study. *SCMS Journal of Indian Management, 2*(4), 95-102.

White, M., Hill, S., McGovern, P., Mills, C. & Smeaton, D. (2003). „High-performance" management practices, working hours and work-life balance. *British Journal of Industrial Relations, 41* (2), 175-195.

Wilk, K. E. (2013). Work-life Balance for Administrators in the Academy: under Ideal Worker Pressure.

Williams, K. & Alliger, G. (1994). Role stressors, mood spillover, and perceptions of work family conflict in employed parents. *Academy of Management Journal, 37* (4), 837-868.

Williams, J. (2000). *Unbending Gender:* Why family and work conflict and what to do about it. New York, NY: Oxford University Press.

Williams, K. J., & Alliger, G. M. (1994). Role stressors, mood spillover, and perceptions of work-family conflict in employed parents. *Academy of Management journal, 37*(4), 837-868.

Winslow, S. (2005). Work-family conflict, gender, and parenthood, 1977-1997. *Journal of Family Issues 26, 727-746.*

Wolf-Wendel, L., Twombly, S. B., Rice, S. (2003). Dual-career-couple hiring policies in higher education. Baltimore, MD: The Johns Hopkins University Press

Wolf-Wendel, L. E. & Ward, K. (2006). Academic life and motherhood: Variations by institutional type. Higher Education, 52,487-521.

Yang, H. L., Kao, Y. H., & Huang, Y. C. (2006). The job self-efficacy and job involvement of clinical nursing teachers. *Journal of Nursing Research, 14*(3), 237-249

Zedeck, S. & Mosier, K. L. (1990). Work in the family and employing organization. *American Psychologist,* 45(2), 240-251.

Zedeck, S. (1992). Introduction: Exploring the domain of work and family concerns. In S. Zedeck (Ed). *Work, families, and organizations* (pp. 1-32). San Francisco, CA: JosseyBass, Inc.

Zedeck, S and Mosier K. (1990) "Work in the Family and Employing Organization', *American Psychologist* 45: 240-51.

done, can go a long way in reducing the conflict, make family domain more flexible and less permeable.